所有的路最终都是回家的路

[美] 约瑟夫·伍德·克鲁奇 等著
张白桦 译

世界微型小说精选
哲理卷（中英双语）

中国国际广播出版社

自 序

微型小说，又名小小说，今天已经成长为一个独立的文体。作为小说"四大家族"之一，微型小说进入"蒲松龄文学奖"和"鲁迅文学奖"的视野，成为当代受众范围最广的纯文学样式。这一成就的取得，与当代外国微型小说的汉译有着直接的关系。对此，我在《当代外国微型小说汉译的翻译文学意义》的论文中有过详尽的阐述。具体说来，这种新型的、活力四射的文学样式的引进，推动了中国当代主流文学重归文学性，重塑了当代主流诗学，提高了文学的地位，从而创造了民族文学史、国别文学史上的"神话"，具有翻译文学意义。

微型小说翻译对于我来说，好像"量身定制"一般。20世纪80年代初，微型小说在中国横空出世，这种简约而不简单的文体非常适合我的审美取向和性格特征，而翻译则可以调动起我全部的知识和双语语言积累。从1987年我发表的第一篇微型小说译作《他活着还是死了》，到2004年的《我是怎样把心丢了的》，这十七年间，我完成的微型小说翻译总计约350万字。

我的微型小说创作有三种：第一种是母语原创，如《白衣女郎》。第二种是汉译英，如在加拿大出版的《中国微型小说精选》（凌鼎年卷），这是中国第一部英译微型小说自选集，我曾参与翻译。第三种是英译汉，这一种类所占比重最大。代表作有《爱旅无涯》《仇家》《爱你至深》等。

我翻译时的期待视野定位在青年身上，目的是做文化、文学的"媒"，因此更愿意贴近读者，特别是青年读者，觉得"大家好才是真的好"。在翻译策略上以归化为主，异化为辅；在翻译方法上以意译为主，直译为辅；在翻译方式上以全译为主，节译为辅；在翻译风格上以时代性为特色，笃信"一代人有一代人的翻译"之说。

所幸这样的取向还是与读者和社会的需求相契合的，因而产生了一定的社会效益。首译都会发表在国内的百强、十佳报刊，如《读者》《中外期刊文萃》《微型小说选刊》《小小说选刊》《青年参考》《文学故事报》等。常见的情况是，在这样的权威报刊发表后，随即就会呈现"凡有井水处，即能歌柳词"的景观，如《爱你至深》发表的二十年间就被转载60余次。

转载不仅限于报刊之间，数十种权威专辑和选本的纸质版也有收录，如《21世纪中国文学大系翻译文学》、《外国微型小说三百篇》、《世界微型小说经典》（8卷）、《世界微型小说名家名作百年经典》（10卷）；电子版图书如《小小说的盛宴书系：别人的女郎》《诺贝尔文学奖获奖作家微型小说精选》等；网上资源如读秀、百链期刊、龙源期刊网等。

此外，众所周知，微型小说历来是中考、高考、四六级的语文和英语考试的听力、阅读理解、翻译、作文的模拟试题和真题材料。微型小说还是影视短剧、喜剧、小品的改编材料。

当然，还有社会影响。第一，多次荣获国家级奖项。1998年《爱旅无涯》获《中国青年报·青年参考》最受读者喜爱的翻译文学作品，2010年当选小小说存档作家，2002年"英汉经典阅读"系列获上海外国语大学学术文化节科研成果奖，2002年当选当代微型小说百家，2002年《译作》当选全国第四次微型小说续写大赛竞赛原作。第二，受到知名评论家张锦贻、陈勇等关注和评论达10余次。第三，曾受邀参加中央电视台、内蒙古电视台及电台、中国作家网的人物专访。第四，个人传记入选美国与捷克出版的《华文微型小说微自传》《中国当代微型小说百家论续集》《世界微型小说百家传论》。第五，因为翻译而收到来自世界各地、各行各业的读者来信、电话、邮件不计其数。

虽然近年我转向长篇小说的翻译，并以《老人与海》《房龙地理》《鹿出没》等再次获得读者的青睐，然而对于我来说，那些年，绞尽脑汁一字一句地写在稿纸上，满怀希冀地一封一封地把译稿投进邮筒，忐忑不安地在报亭、邮局一本一本地翻找自己的译作，欢天喜地买几本回家，进门就问女儿"Can you guess?"等她的固定答案"妈妈又发了！"都是我生命中一个一个的定格瞬间。微型小说翻译是我的"初心",而唯有"初心"是不能辜负的。因此,我于2015年开办了以我的微型小说翻译为内容的自媒体——微型公众号"白桦译林",收获了大量读者和转载,更促成了"译趣坊·世界微型小说精选"系列的陆续出版。

  谨以此书感谢多年来扶持过我的报刊编辑老师,以及多年来一直乐于阅读我的微型小说的读者和学生。

目 录

content

午夜的不速之客 / Midnight Visitor · 1

欢迎来抢我们银行 / Welcome to Our Bank · 10

所有的路,最终都是回家的路 / All Roads Lead Home · 17

特殊的听众 / A Different Kind of Audience · 21

甜蜜的谎言 / Sweet Lies · 23

贼 / Thief · 32

一小时的故事 / The Story of an Hour · 41

怎么对待生活 / How to Handle Life · 50

你是什么人,你已经出卖了自己 / You Tell on Yourself · 52

心与手 / Hearts and Hands · 56

一个简单的建议 / A Simple Proposition · 63

你恰逢其时 / You Are Very Much on Time · 70

初雪 / The First Snow · 74

仇恨 / Hate · 76

一扇关上的门 / A Closed Door · 82

令人脑洞大开的墓志铭 / Epitaph · 87

什么属于你 / What Was Mine · 89

足球大赛 / The Big Match · 93

蓝宝石项链 / A String of Blue Beaks · 98

学艺的正确打开方式 / Patience to Learn · 107

致讨厌我的人的一封信 / To Haters · 110

机票 / The Ticket · 113

爱情信使 / By Courier · 119

爱与喜欢 / Love and Like · 129

在路上 / We Are on a Journey · 131

时间是什么 / What Is Time · 133

半英里 / The Half Mile · 135

星座决定性格 / Constellations Determine Character · 168

跟汪星人学做人 / If a Dog Were Your Teacher · 176

接触的人越多，发现自己越喜欢狗 / A Tribute to the Dog · 180

令人难以置信的真实 / The Unbelievably Truth · 184

人一辈子能活几次 / How Many Lives Do You Have · 188

我不再想要我的静静 / The New Silence · 190

山顶小屋 / The House on the Hill · 195

午夜的不速之客

约瑟夫·伍德·克鲁奇

奥赛布尔的长相与佛勒所读到过的关于密探的描述全都对不上号。佛勒跟在奥赛布尔后面,走在阴暗的法国旅馆走廊里,心里很是失望。奥赛布尔租的是在这家旅馆六层楼上的一个小房间,完全不像是一个浪漫人物住的地方。

奥赛布尔是个胖子,大胖子,这是其一。其二,他说话有口音。虽然他法语和德语都讲得也还马马虎虎,但二十年前他从波士顿带到巴黎来的新英格兰口音却依然会露出马脚。

"你失望了吧?"奥赛布尔回头说,"你听说我是特工,是间谍,从事谍报和危险工作。你之所以希望见我是因为你是个年轻而又浪漫的作家。你原以为可以看到夜色中的神秘人物,听见几声噼噼啪啪的枪声,看到葡萄酒里面下的药。

"没想到却跟一个邋遢的胖子在一家法国音乐厅里面无聊乏味地过了一个晚上,没看到有乌黑眼睛的美女悄悄地把情报塞进他手里,只不过接到了一个普普通通的约好在他屋里见面的电话。真是太没劲啦!"胖子一边自顾自轻声地笑着,一边打开房门,侧身让客人先进去。

"你的幻想破灭了,不过,打起精神来,年轻的朋友,"奥赛布尔对他说,"待会儿你会看到一份文件,一份非常重要的文件,为了得到这份文件,好几个男女已经冒了生命危险。在送到我这里来以后就会最终送到官方的手里。这份文件完全可能在未来的某一天影响历史的进程。这么一想就很有戏剧性了吧?"奥赛布尔说着,随手上了门,然后打开了灯。

灯一亮,佛勒这一天头一次真的大吃一惊:屋子中央站着一个人,手里握着一把小巧的自动手枪。

奥赛布尔眨了眨眼睛。"麦克斯,"他气喘吁吁地说道,"你可把我吓了一大跳。我以为你在柏林呢。你在我房间里干什么?"

麦克斯瘦瘦的,个子不高,长着一张让人一看就会联想到狐狸的脸。要不是手上拿着枪,他看上去危险性并不高。"那份报告,"他低声说道,"那份今晚将送到你这儿来的关于新式导弹的报告,我想从你这儿拿走。在我手里比在你手里更安全。"

奥赛布尔走到一把扶手椅跟前重重地一屁股坐了下去。"这一次我非得跟这里的管理部门好好说道说道了,也太让我生气了。"他态度严肃地说道,"这已经是这个月来有人第二次从那个该死的阳台上闯进我的房间了。"佛勒的目光投向房间唯一的一扇窗户。那是一扇普普通通的窗户,窗外夜色正浓,阴森森的。

"阳台?"麦克斯问道。"不,我有万能钥匙。我不知道有阳台。我要是早知道的话,就不会那么麻烦啦。"

"那本来不是我的阳台,"奥赛布尔扫了佛勒一眼,气呼呼地解释说,"是隔壁那个套间的。跟你说吧,这个房间原本是一个大套间的一部分,隔壁房间,通过那扇门,原来是一个起居室,这个起居室带阳台,阳台现在延伸到我的窗下面。你可以从隔壁那空着的房间到阳台上去,上个月就有人那样干过。管理人员答应把它封起来的,可是到现在还没封。"

麦克斯扫了佛勒一眼,只见佛勒直挺挺地站在距离奥赛布尔几英尺的地方。"请你坐下来,"麦克斯用命令的姿势晃了晃手中的枪,对佛勒说道,"我们还要等半个钟头呢!"

"三十一分钟。"奥赛布尔闷闷不乐地说道。"约会定在十二点半。我真想知道你们德国人是怎么知道这份报告的,麦克斯。"奥赛布尔说道。

小个子特工阴险地笑了,"我们也真想知道你们的人是怎么搞到这份报告的呢。不过,还没造成什么危害。今晚我就要把它拿回去了。怎么回事?门外是什么人?"听到突如其来的敲门声,佛勒吓得跳了起来。

奥赛布尔只是微微一笑,"是警察,"他说,"我考虑到这么重要的文件应该有点儿额外的保护措施,于是就事先跟他们打了声招呼,让他们来查看一下,以确保万无一失。"

麦克斯紧张地咬着嘴唇。敲门声再次响起。

"现在你打算怎么办,麦克斯?"奥赛布尔问道。"就是我不去开门,他们也照样会进来,门没有锁。而且,他们会毫不迟疑地开枪。"

麦克斯气得脸色铁青,迅速向窗口退去;他伸出一只手从身后打开窗户,把一条腿伸到漆黑的窗外。"把他们支走!"他警告说,"我在阳台上等着,把他们支走,不然,我就开枪碰碰我的运气啦!"

敲门声越来越响,而且,一个声音高叫着,"奥赛布尔先生!奥赛布尔先生!"

在窗口的那个人扭着身子,以便枪口能仍对着胖子和他的客人,接着,他将另一条腿摆起来甩过了窗台。

门把手转动了。麦克斯飞快地用左手一撑,跳到阳台上。接着,他落下去的时候,尖利刺耳地叫了一声。

门开了,只见一名侍应生端着一个托盘、一瓶酒和两个玻璃杯,站在门口。"这是您要的饮料,先生。"他将托盘放到桌上,把瓶塞拔掉就离开了房间。

佛勒面色苍白,浑身发抖,瞪大眼睛目送着侍应生离去的背影。"可……可是……警……察呢?"他结结巴巴地问道。

"压根儿就没有什么警察。"奥赛布尔叹了口气,说道,"只有亨利,我就是在等亨利。"

"可是阳台上的那个人呢?"佛勒还要往下问。

"他呀,"奥赛布尔说,"他回不来了,你看,我年轻的朋友,这里没有阳台。"

Midnight Visitor

By Joseph Wood Krutch

Ausable did not fit the description of any secret agent Fowler had ever read about. Following him down the corridor of the gloomy French hotel where Ausable had a room, Fowler felt disappointed. It was a small room on the sixth floor and hardly a setting for a romantic figure.

Ausable was, for one thing, fat. Very fat. And then there was his accent. Though he spoke French and German passably, he had never altogether lost New England accent he had brought to Paris from Boston twenty years ago.

"You are disappointed," Ausable said wheezily over his shoulder. "You were told that I was a secret agent, a spy, dealing in espionage and danger. You wished to meet me because you are a writer, young and romantic. You thought you would have mysterious figures in the night, the crack of pistols, drugs in the wine.

"Instead, you have spent a dull evening in a French music

hall with a sloppy fat man who, instead of having messages slipped into his hand by dark-eyed beauties, gets only an ordinary telephone call making an appointment in his room. You have been bored!" The fat man chuckled to himself as he unlocked the door of his room and stood aside to let his frustrated guest enter.

"You are disillusioned," Ausable told him. "But take cheer, my young friend. Before long you will see a paper, a quite important paper for which several men and women have risked their lives, come to me in the next-to-last step of its journey into official hands. Some day soon that paper may well affect the course of history. There is drama in that thought, don't you think?" As he spoke, Ausable closed the door behind him. Then he switched on the light.

And as the light came on, Fowler had his first real thrill of the day. For halfway across the room, a small automatic pistol in his hand, stood a man.

Ausable blinked a few times. "Max," he wheezed, "you gave me quite a start. I thought you were in Berlin. What are you doing in my room?"

Max was slender, not tall, and with a face that suggested the look of a fox. Except for the gun, he did not look very dangerous.

"The report," he murmured. "The report that is being brought to you tonight concerning some new missiles. I thought I would take it from you. It will be safer in my hands than in yours."

Ausable moved to an armchair and sat down heavily. "I'm going to raise the devil with the management this time; I am angry." he said grimly. "This is the second time in a month that somebody has gotten into my room off that confounded balcony!" Fowler's eyes went to the single window of the room. It was an ordinary window, against which now the night was pressing blackly.

"Balcony?" Max asked curiously. "No, I had a passkey. I did not know about the balcony. It might have saved me some trouble had I known about it."

"It's not my balcony," explained Ausable angrily. "It belongs to the next apartment." He glanced explanatorily at Fowler. "You see," he said, "this room used to be part of a large unit, and the next room through that door there used to be the living room. It had the balcony, which extends under my window now. You can get onto it from the empty room next door, and somebody did, last month. The management promised to block it off. But they haven't."

Max glanced at Fowler, who was standing stiffly a few feet from Ausable, and waved the gun with a commanding gesture. "Please sit down," he said. "We have a wait of half an hour, I think."

"Thirty-one minutes," Ausable said moodily. "The appointment was for twelve thirty. I wish I knew how you learned about the report, Max."

The little spy smiled evilly. "And we wish we knew how your people got the report. But, no harm has been done. I will get it back tonight. What is that? Who is at the door?" Fowler jumped at the sudden knocking at the door.

Ausable just smiled, "That will be the police," he said. "I thought that such an important paper should have a little extra protection. I told them to check on me to make sure everything was all right."

Max bit his lip nervously. The knocking was repeated.

"What will you do now, Max?" Ausable asked. "If I do not answer the door, they will enter anyway. The door is unlocked. And they will not hesitate to shoot."

Max's face was black with anger as he backed swiftly toward the window; with his hand behind him, he opened the window and put his leg out into the night. "Send them away!" he warned. "I will wait on the balcony. Send them away or I'll shoot and take my chances!"

The knocking at the door became louder and a voice was raised. "Mr. Ausable! Mr. Ausable!"

Keeping his body twisted so that his gun still covered the fat man and his guest, the man at the window swung his other leg up and over the window sill.

The doorknob turned. Swiftly Max pushed with his left hand

to free himself and drop to the balcony. And then as he dropped, he screamed once, shrilly.

The door opened and a waiter stood there with a tray, a bottle and two glasses. "Here is the drink you ordered, sir." He set the tray on the table, uncorked the bottle, and left the room.

White faced and shaking, Fowler stared after him. "But…but…what about…the police?" he stammered.

"There never were any police." Ausable sighed. "Only Henry, whom I was expecting."

"But what about the man on the balcony?" Fowler began.

"No," said Ausable, "he won't return. You see, my young friend, there is no bacony."

欢迎来抢我们银行

"我真希望中央银行被抢劫。"乔治·皮肯斯自言自语道。自从他当上这家银行的出纳的那一天起,他就天天这么盼望着。

全国的银行都被抢了个遍,怎么单单不抢这家银行呢?他越想越不是滋味儿。难道强盗们对这里400万美元的现金不屑一顾吗?还是他们怕这里的老警卫阿克门先生?可是他已经22年没掏出过他的枪了。

当然,乔治有理由盼望这个银行被抢劫。毕竟,他不可能把他从早到晚经手的大捆钞票就这么拿走。于是,他想出了另一个法子把它们弄到手。他的计划很简单,大致如下:

假如强盗甲劫持了银行出纳员乙……假设乙把一定数额的钱交给了强盗甲……

那么又有什么能阻止乙把剩下的钱全部私吞,然后就说所有的钱都被甲抢走了呢?关键问题只有一个,强盗甲在哪儿?

一天早晨,乔治走进银行时觉得似乎要出事。"早上好,伯罗斯先生。"他兴高采烈地跟经理打招呼,经理嘀咕了什么就走进了自己的办公室。

两点钟的时候,强盗甲走进了银行。乔治一眼就看出他是抢银行的强盗,原因之一是他进来时鬼鬼祟祟,二是他戴着面罩。

"抢劫!"那家伙大喊大叫。他从口袋里掏出手枪。警卫那儿传来一点儿响动。"你，"强盗说道："趴在地上！"阿克门先生趴下了。强盗走到乔治的窗口前。

"好了，把钱交出来！"

"是，先生。"乔治答应着。"你要10元一张的还是20元一张的？"

"只管交出来就是！"

乔治把手伸进装现金的盒子，把顶层的钞票都拿了出来——有6000元左右。他把钱从窗口递出来。强盗一把抓住钱塞进口袋，转身就跑。

当大家都盯着强盗甲的时候，出纳乙沉着地挪开出纳箱上层的钞票，把盒子里下层的钞票偷偷塞进了自己的口袋。

强盗逃之夭夭。乔治昏了过去。当他醒来时，朝那一张张焦急地瞧着他的脸微笑。"我没事儿。"他勇敢地说。

"也许你应该回家了，乔治。"首席审计员贝尔先生说道。

乔治刚刚安全地走进自己的卧室，就在门后，从口袋里掏出钱来数。他有7000美元了，他不禁欢天喜地起来。

第二天早晨，乔治来到银行。银行没有营业，但全体职员都来了，正在协助贝尔先生进行特别审计、审核、查账。

乔治被叫进了伯罗斯先生的办公室。让他感到意外的是，这位银行经理似乎很高兴。"乔治，"他说，"我想让你见一下我们银行的前任经理卡拉瑟斯先生。"

"早上好，乔治，"卡拉瑟斯先生说，"听说你昨天晕倒了，我很难过。你现在好了吗？"

"好了，先生，全好了，谢谢！"

"听到你这么说，我很高兴。那确实是非同一般的冒险，这件事说明抢劫咱们银行易如反掌！"

"先生,您是什么意思?"乔治大惑不解。

"乔治,很抱歉昨天让你受苦了。因为近来所有银行都遭到了抢劫,我觉得想个办法证明一下咱们的小银行也会被抢,是个好主意。我已经退休了,可我并没停止思考。所以,昨天我搞了个小游戏,只不过是为了让每个人都提高警惕。"

"我不明白,"乔治说,"什么游戏?"

这位老人哈哈大笑,嗖地一下拿出一个面具戴在自己脸上,说道:"好,把钱交出来!"伯罗斯先生哈哈大笑起来,乔治可笑不出来。

"那钱呢?"乔治低声问道。

"别担心,"卡拉瑟斯先生说道,"我已经把钱全放回你的出纳箱里了,一共6000元。现在,我们就要查完账了。"乔治吓得浑身冰凉。

他们身后那扇门开了,首席审计员贝尔先生把头伸了进来。"伯罗斯先生,"他态度严肃地说,"你能出来一下吗?"

Welcome to Our Bank

"I wish Central Bank would be robbed," George Pickens said to himself. He had been making this wish daily from the time he had started work as a teller at the bank.

All over the country banks were being robbed, George thought sourly. Why not this bank? Were robbers scornful of its four-million-dollar capital? Were they afraid of Mr. Ackerman, the old bank guard, who hadn't pulled out his gun in twenty-two years?

Of course, George had a reason for wanting the bank to be robbed. After all, he couldn't simply take the thick bundles of bills that were under his hands all day long. So he had thought of another way to get them. His plan was simple. It went like this:

If Bank Robber A holds up Bank Teller B…And if Bank Teller B gives Bank Robber A a certain amount of money…

What is to prevent Bank Teller B from keeping all the money left and claiming that it was stolen by Bank Robber A? There was only one problem. Where was Bank Robber A?

One morning George entered the bank feeling something

was about to happen. "Good morning, Mr. Burrows." he said cheerfully. The bank president muttered something and went into his office.

At two o'clock Bank Robber A walked in. George knew he was a bank robber. For one thing, he slunk in. For another thing, he wore a mask.

"This is a holdup!" the man said roughly. He took a pistol from his pocket. The guard made a small sound. "You," the bank robber said, "lie down on the floor." Mr. Ackerman lay down. The robber stepped over to George's cage.

"All right." he said. "Hand it over."

"Yes, sir." said George. "Would you like it in ten or twenty dollar bills?"

"Just hand it over!"

George reached into his cashbox and took all the bills from the top section, close to six thousand dollars. He passed them through the window. The robber snatched them, stuffed them into his pocket, and turned to leave.

Then, while everyone watched Bank Robber A, Bank Teller B calmly lifted off the top section of the cashbox and slipped bills from the bottom section into his pockets.

The bank robber was gone. George fainted. When he woke he smiled up at the worried faces looking down at him. "I'm all right." he said bravely.

"Perhaps you should go home, George." Mr. Bell, the chief auditor, said.

As soon as he was safely behind his bedroom door, George took the money from his pockets and counted it. He had seven thousand dollars. He was very happy.

The next morning when George arrived at the bank, it was not open for business. But everyone was there, helping to examine the bank's records for the special audit Mr. Bell was taking.

George was called into Mr. Burrows's office. The bank president seemed strangely cheerful. "George," he said, "I want you to meet Mr. Carruthers, who used to be president of our bank."

"Good morning, George." said Mr. Carruthers. "I was sorry to hear you fainted yesterday. Are you all right now?"

"Yes, sir. Just fine, thanks."

"I'm glad to hear it. That was quite an adventure. It just goes to show how easy it is to rob our bank."

"Sir?" said George, confused.

"George, I was sorry to give you a hard time yesterday, but with all the banks being robbed these days I thought it would be a good idea to prove that our little bank can be robbed too. I have retired, but I haven't stopped thinking. That's why I played my little game yesterday, just to keep everybody on his toes."

"I don't understand." said George. "What game?"

The old man laughed and whipped out a mask. He placed it

over his face and said, "All right. Hand it over!" Mr. Burrows laughed but George did not.

"And the money?" George asked in a small voice.

"Don't worry." Mr. Carruthers said. "I put it all back in your cashbox, all six thousand. We're just finishing up the audit now." George turned cold with fear.

Behind them, the door opened and Mr. Bell, the chief auditor, put his head into the room. "Mr.Burrows," he said gravely, "may I see you a moment?"

所有的路，最终都是回家的路

当我还是个小男孩的时候，没有智能电话、电脑，也没有什么东西能够播放"星球大战"，电视只有一个频道是清楚的。即使这样，我也不觉得无聊。家附近的田野、山坡、林地都是完美的玩耍场所，只有想不到，没有玩不到的探险活动。

我还记得有次徒步去附近的一个湖，我沿着湖边慢慢地走着，在湖的后面，我惊奇地发现了一条之前从来没有见过的年代久远的窄小土路。我当即就决定去走走。这条路上遍布凹坑以及泥巴上的轮胎印记，在路的两边类似分界线般的深山老林，可是这样的探索似乎就像一场精彩的探险。

我走啊走，可能已经走了好几个小时，守护我安全的小天使在我耳边低语，让我掉头回家，可是我执拗，甚至显得有些愚蠢，依旧继续往前走。

走着走着，土路渐渐变成了砂石路，又慢慢变成了平路，但是目力所及之处未见汽车和房子。我的双腿走乏了。我注意到太阳也开始落山了，我开始害怕起来，我不想等天黑以后困在这条路上，但是如果现在往回走的话，我可以肯定在天黑前也回不到湖边。

我继续朝前走着，恐惧在我心中愈演愈烈，心在狂跳，双腿疼痛。在我拐最后一个弯时，看见远处好像有什么东西，我认出那是一幢房子，我的泪水几乎夺眶而出。

  我的心怦怦直跳！我又蹦又跳，哈哈大笑。我认得这就是回家的路啊！尽管还要一英里才能到家，我的腿却像羽毛般轻快，我急急忙忙地赶回了家。我笑容满面地走进家来，正好赶上晚上的饭点。饭后，我的冒险以晚上的一夜酣睡完美收官。

  我记得最近见过的一则标语是这样说的："所有的路，最终都是回家的路。"此言不虚，这辈子所有的路不管怎样迂回曲折，最终都会引导着我们回家，有的是回到我们物质层面的家，有的是回到我们心灵的家园。

  愿你的人生之路都有爱为伴，愿你在旅途中帮助同路人，愿你人生中的一段又一段旅程都是通往回"家"的路。

All Roads Lead Home

When I was a boy there were no smart phones, computers were something you saw on STAR TREK, and our television only got one channel clearly. Still, I was never bored. The fields, hills, and woodlands around my home were the perfect playground whose adventures were only limited by my imagination.

I can remember once hiking to a nearby lake and slowly walking around it. At the backside of it I was amazed to find an old, one lane, dirt road that I had never seen before. I immediately set out to travel it. It was full of potholes and muddy tire tracks and deep woods bordered it on both sides, but exploring it still seemed like a fine adventure.

I walked on and on for what seemed like hours. I am sure my guardian angel was whispering in my ear to turn around and head back home but I was stubborn and even a bit stupid, so I walked on.

The dirt road gave way to a gravel one and then a paved one, yet there was still neither a car nor a house in sight. My legs were getting tired. I noticed that the sun was starting to go down and I grew scared. I didn't want to end up trapped on this road in the dark of night, but I was sure it would be dark before I could make my way back to the lake again.

I continued to walk on with the fear growing inside of me. My heart was pounding and my legs were aching. I was almost in tears when I turned one last curve and saw something in the distance. It was a house that I recognized.

My heart leapt up! I jumped up and down and laughed out loud. I knew the way home! It was still over a mile away but my legs felt like feathers and I hurried back to my house in no time. I walked in with a big smile on my face just in time for dinner. Then I ended my adventure with a good night's sleep.

I remembered this recently when I saw a sign that said: "All roads lead Home." This is true. In this life all roads no matter what their twists and turns can lead us home again. They can lead us to our homes here on Earth. They can lead us to our homes in our hearts.

May you always walk your path with love. May you always help your fellow travelers along the way. And may your roads always lead you Home again.

特殊的听众

阿尔·史密斯是个名人，出生在纽约市东区的一个贫寒的家庭，担任过纽约州的州长。他没文化，却努力经营，最终爬上了高位。

有一天，他以州长的身份参观了纽约辛辛监狱。辛辛监狱是美国最大的监狱之一。监狱长请史密斯给因犯们讲几句话。史密斯先生以前从来没有给犯人讲过话，他不知道该怎么称呼他们。

最后，他终于开了口："我亲爱的公民们……"接着他想起被收监服刑的人已经不再是公民了。他改口道："我亲爱的囚犯们……"这听起来也不对头，于是他索性省略了称谓，说道："嗯，不管怎样，今天在这里见到你们这么多人，我很高兴。"

A Different Kind of Audience

Al Smith was governor of New York State. He was a famous man. He was born very poor on the East Side of New York City. He was devoid of culture, but he worked very hard and reached positions of great power.

One day, as governor, he was visiting the state prison at Sing-Sing. Sing-Sing is one of the largest prisons in the United States. The head of the prison asked Mr. Smith to say something to the prisoners. Mr. Smith had never spoken to this kind of audience before. He did not know how to begin.

Finally, he said, "My fellow citizens…" Then he remembered that when a man goes to prison he is no longer a citizen. He began again, "My fellow prisoners…" That did not sound right, so he said: "Well, anyway, I'm glad to see so many of you here today."

甜蜜的谎言

劳拉·基恩·贝克

我在八年级前的那个夏天从马萨诸塞州搬到了北卡罗来纳州。没过多久,我就发现我的新同学比我的老朋友对约会更感兴趣。公共汽车上的女孩不断地谈论谁和谁"在一起"。起初我不知道她们的意思。十二岁或十三岁就有男朋友了?我完全没有准备好!

然而,当听到别人的爱情生活时,我却还是全神贯注地听着。一个名叫加思的男孩是八卦的一个主要对象。每隔一天,就会有一个流言说他和一个新的女孩出去。他比我低一个年级,但是他跟我坐同一趟公共汽车,所以我知道他是谁。他金发碧眼,可爱,为人八面玲珑。我觉得他太自恋了,但我可以看出他受欢迎的原因。

加思似乎从来没有注意到我。我没指望他会注意到我——我是一个新来的孩子,一个书呆子,没有大多数人所说的漂亮容貌。所以,当他在二月份的一天往我家给我打电话时,我感到大吃一惊。他打电话说他喜欢我。非常喜欢。喜欢我!

一两天以后,他在公共汽车上坐在我的后排,开始用一种安静、严肃的声音说话。他谈起他自己,谈起他以前的艰苦生活。

"小时候我们家经常搬家,"他说道,"所以我从来没有过最好的朋友。也许正因为如此，我一直是一个孤独的人。我可以在外面表现得很友好，但我总是隐藏我内心深处的真实。"

说着，他靠近我。"我想我只是太敏感了。"他说道。"我觉得世事，我认为世事真的很难……所以，我不想让人们靠近我。"

我下了公共汽车，心里想着自己以往对加思真的不够公平。他并不是傲慢。那只是他示人的面具，所以人们不知道他内心有多敏感。我为他感到难过。他是如此善良——又是如此不幸！

几天之后，加思放学后来到我家，我们站在门廊上谈了很长时间。天气很冷，但我们不在乎。实际上，我们根本没有注意到。我们谈得太投入了。

"我得告诉你，"他说道，"我想我爱上你了。你真是太棒了，太完美了——"

"不，我不是！"我说着，绯红了脸。

"你是！"他坚持说着。"你很漂亮，你彬彬有礼……"

我不善于应对恭维，即使我知道对方说的是真的。而当对方说的不是真的的时候，我希望它们是真的……"我不漂亮。"我说。"我连可爱都谈不上。"

"你漂亮。"加思说道。他用手臂搂住我。这感觉很奇怪，但我没有试着去阻止他。"听着，"他说道，"我和很多女孩一起出去过，我知道。但是，你很特别。你真的很特别。"

我摇摇头，但我没有试图争辩。

"听着，"加思说道。"我跟你说，要是你能帮助我让我不再那么敏感的话，我会帮你让你不再总是自黑。好吗？"

我朝他笑了笑。"好吧，"我说道。

他把我搂紧了些，低下头，好像要吻我似的。我不知道该怎么办。

我突然转过头去，他的脸只是拂过我的脸颊。我觉得有点儿笨拙，但我很高兴他没吻上。我还没准备好接吻，我真的不喜欢他那样。

我觉得头脑里一片混乱。我既高兴又兴奋还有些受宠若惊，但还是觉得有点儿不对劲儿。一方面，当我并不是真的爱他的时候，我觉得我在假装爱他，难道我不应该告诉他真相吗？可是怎么告诉他呢？而他又怎么可能爱上我呢？他几乎都不怎么了解我！

就在这时，我妈妈打开外面的灯，加思迅速放开了我。他说道："明天见！"然后就沿着那条路走了。

在房子外面待了那么长时间以后，在房子里感到闷热和温暖。我把书丢在厨房里，一溜烟儿跑回卧室来理清思绪。

我真的只愿意让加思成为一个朋友，但是在他的手臂里的感觉很好。有人爱上我也是挺酷的。我告诉自己，我不需要做任何事情。除了一起消磨时光，管他和别人"在一起"是什么意思，我只要告诉他我还没准备好接吻，可以吗？

第二天，在公交车上，加思好像我们之间什么也没发生过似的。他表现得我们只是朋友。我告诉自己，他想淡化它，这样其他孩子就不会取笑我们了。但他的演技似乎有点儿太好了。

在接下来的几天里，每当我们独处的时候，加思就说他有多爱我。但当其他人在场时，他表现得我们只是朋友。当然，我只是和他交朋友，但整件事都开始困扰我了。他为喜欢我而感到羞耻吗？还是他一开始就撒了谎？他为什么要撒谎？

一个星期过去了，在这之后，我几乎没有看到加思。没关系。我其实也并不想念他。我对他很困惑，对所发生的事情和它的意义感到困惑。大约一个月后，我听到了一些有助我理解的消息。

当时我在公交车上，听见一个女孩提到加思的名字。"真恶心。"

她说道。"他们实际上在吹嘘自己亲吻过多少女孩!当然,加思的数字最多。"

"是的,"她的朋友说。"比如,学校里每一个七年级和八年级的女生他都吻过!我听说他现在在九年级的女生身上下功夫。"

我觉得我的肚子被狠狠地踹了一脚似的。我只是想爬到座位下死去。我怎么会这么蠢呢?我怎么能相信他那些荒谬的谎言呢?

过了一会儿,我最终缓了过来。毕竟,他骗了很多女孩,不只是我。我只是希望我能听到内心的声音,说出了点儿差错。现在我更清楚了。我知道你应该永远都聆听内心那个低低的警告的声音,因为它通常是正确的。

Sweet Lies

By Laura Gene Beck

I moved from Massachusetts to North Carolina the summer before eighth grade. It didn't take me long to notice that my new classmates were a lot more interested in dating than my old friends had been. Girls on the bus continually talked about who was "going with" who. At first I didn't know what they meant. Having a boyfriend at twelve or thirteen? I was totally not ready for that!

Still, I was all ears when it came to other people's love lives. A boy named Garth was a major subject of gossip. Every other day, the rumors had him going out with a different girl. He was a year behind me, but he rode my bus so I knew who he was. He was blond and cute and very smooth. I thought he was a little too in love with himself, but I could see why he was popular.

Garth never seemed to pay much attention to me. Not that I expected him to—I was a new kid, sort of a nerd and not what most people would call pretty. So I was totally surprised when he called me up at home one day in February. He called to say he liked me. A lot. Me!

A day or two later, he took the seat behind me on the bus and started talking in a quiet, serious voice. He talked about himself, about the hard life he'd had.

"We moved a lot when I was a kid," he said. "So I never had a best friend. And maybe because of that, I've always been a loner. I can act friendly on the outside, but I always keep the real, deep parts of me hidden."

He leaned closer to me. "I guess I'm just too sensitive," he said. "I feel things, I take things really hard…so, I don't want people to get close."

I got off the bus thinking that I hadn't really been fair to Garth. He wasn't stuck up. That was just a face he put on, so people wouldn't know how sensitive he was. I felt sorry for him. He was so nice—and so unhappy!

A few days after that, Garth came by my house after school. We stood around on my porch talking for a long time. It was cold, but we didn't care. Actually, we didn't notice. We were too involved in our conversation.

"I have to tell you," he said. "I think I'm falling in love with you. You're just so amazing, so perfect—"

"No, I'm not!" I said, blushing.

"You are!" he insisted. "You're beautiful, you have great manners…"

I'm not good with compliments even when I know they're true. But when they're not true, and I wish they were... "I'm not beautiful," I said. "I'm not even pretty."

"You are beautiful," said Garth. He put his arm around me. It felt strange, but I didn't try to stop him. "Look," he said. "I've gone with a lot of girls, and I know. You're special. You really are."

I shook my head, but I didn't try to argue.

"Listen," said Garth. "Tell you what—I'll help you stop saying bad things about yourself, if you'll help me stop being so sensitive. Okay?"

I smiled at him. "Okay," I said.

He held me closer and bent his head like he was going to kiss me. I didn't know what to do. I turned away suddenly, and his face just brushed my cheek. I felt kind of clumsy, but I was glad he'd missed. I wasn't ready for kissing, and I honestly didn't like him "that way".

I felt all mixed up inside. I was happy and excited and totally flattered, but something still felt wrong. For one thing, I felt like I was pretending to love him when I really didn't. Shouldn't I tell him the truth? But how? And how could he be in love with me, anyway? He hardly knew me!

Just then my mom turned on the outside light, and Garth let go of me fast. He said, "See you tomorrow!" and took off down the road.

The house felt stuffy and warm after all that time outside. I dropped my books in the kitchen and ran up to my bedroom to think.

I really only liked Garth as a friend, but his arm did feel nice around me. And it was kind of cool having someone in love with me. I told myself it wasn't like I had to do anything about it. What did "going out" with someone mean anyway, besides just spending time together? I could just tell him I wasn't ready for kissing—couldn't I?

The next day on the bus, Garth acted like nothing had happened between us. He acted like we were just friends. I told myself he wanted to play it down so the other kids wouldn't tease us. But his acting seemed a little too good.

For the next few days, whenever we were alone, Garth talked about how he loved me. But when other people were around, he acted like we were just friends. Of course, I was just friends with him, but the whole thing was starting to bother me. Was he ashamed of liking me? Or was he lying about it in the first place? Why would he lie?

A week went by, and after that, I hardly saw Garth at all. That was okay. I didn't exactly miss him. I was so confused about him, about what had happened and about what it meant. Then about a month later, I heard something that helped me understand.

I was on the bus when I heard a girl mention Garth's name. "It's disgusting," she said. "They actually brag about how many girls they've kissed! Garth's got the most, of course."

"Yeah," said her friend. "Like every seventh-and eighth-grade girl in the school! I hear he's working on the ninth-graders now."

I felt like I'd been hit in the stomach. I just wanted to crawl under the seat and die. How could I have been so stupid? How could I have believed a single one of his ridiculous lies?

It took me a while, but eventually I got over it. After all, he fooled a lot of girls, not just me. I just wished I'd listened to that voice in my head that said something was wrong. Now I know better. I know that you should always listen to that little warning voice, because it's usually right.

贼

他第一次注意到那个年轻女人,是在他到航空公司售票处排队买票的时候。她的乌黑发亮的一头秀发在脑后紧紧地盘成一个结。他想象着那头秀发披散开来瀑布般落在腰间的情形,只见那个女人穿着皮外套的肩上挎着一个沉甸甸的黑色坤包,脚上穿着一双黑色软皮靴。他竭力想看到她的脸,她就排在他的前面。但是,一直到她买好票走开,他才得以一睹她的芳容:雪白的皮肤,乌黑发亮的眼睛,丰满的嘴唇,让他心跳加速。那年轻女人似乎察觉到他在注视着她,便突然垂下了眼睛。

售票员的话打断了他的遐想。他不再看那女人——他想她可能有二十五岁左右——然后买了一张到一个东部城市的二等往返机票。

飞机过一个小时才会起飞。为了消磨时间,他踱进机场的一家鸡尾酒吧,要了一杯兑水的苏格兰威士忌。他一边慢慢地喝着酒,一边望着大厅里川流不息的乘客——他想,其中一定有好多都是未婚的漂亮女人,她们穿的是时装杂志上介绍的那种衣服——直到后来他又瞥见那个穿皮外套的黑发姑娘。她站在旅客服务台旁边,和另一个姑娘聊得正欢。另外那个姑娘金发碧眼,身穿一件镶着灰色毛皮的布外套。不知怎么的,他想引起黑发姑娘的注意,想趁这个姑娘要乘的班机还没起飞之前,请她喝上一杯。然而,尽管他认为她向他这边张望了一小会儿,但他在酒吧的阴暗的地方,吸引不了她的目光。过了没多大一会儿,这两个女人就分手了，都没有朝这个方向走来。他又要了一杯兑水的苏格兰威士忌。

当他再次看见她的时候，他正在买一本杂志，准备在旅途中看。突然，他觉得有人挨近了他。他先是吃了一惊，怎么会有人靠得这么近，都碰到他的身体呢？但等看清是谁之后，他的脸上泛起了笑意。

"这地方人可真多。"他说道。

她抬眼看着他——她是羞红了脸吗？——她的嘴角掠过一丝奇怪的表情，随即就消失了。她从他的身边走开，淹没在大厅的人流之中。

他拿着杂志站在柜台边，但当他将手伸进后边的口袋拿钱包的时候，发现里边已经空空如也了。他想着：我大概是在什么地方把它弄丢的呢？他开始在脑海里清点装在钱包里的信用卡、钞票、会员证、身份证等东西。一种酷似恐惧的感觉使他的胃部剧烈地痉挛起来。那个姑娘挨我那样近，他想——他随即明白了，是她偷了他的钱包。

他可怎么办呢？飞机票还在，装在上衣内袋里万无一失——他把手伸到衣服里面，摸了摸装机票的纸袋，确认了一下。他可以乘这班飞机，到达目的地，叫人来接。他连坐公共汽车的钱都没有了。办完事之后，再乘飞机回家。但是，在此期间要对那些信用卡失窃采取措施——要打电话给家里，让妻子把放在写字台最上面抽屉里的信用卡号码取出来，和信用卡公司通电话——真是麻烦死了，要全部办完，准会要命。他可怎么办呢？

首先，找警察把事情经过以及那年轻女人的模样告诉他。这女人真可恶，好像对他很有意思，站得离他是那样近，听他说话时她羞红的脸是那么娇俏——却一直在处心积虑地要偷他的东西。原来她脸红不是因为害羞，而是做贼心虚。这是最可恨的。这些该死的骗子尤物。这些细节还是不给警察说好——只讲她所做的事情、他的钱包里有什么东西就行了。他咬牙切齿。很可能他再也见不到自己的钱包了。

他正在考虑为了节省时间,就跟那个站在金属探测器旁边的保安员谈一下。突然,他大吃一惊,喜出望外——看到了那个黑发女人靠着大厅的前窗坐着。在她身后渐浓的暮色中,出租车和私家车在缓缓地移动。她好像在全神贯注地看书。她旁边的座位空着。于是,他坐了下来。

"我一直在找你。"他说道。

她瞟了他一眼,似乎没有认出他是谁。"我不认识你。"她说道。

"你肯定会认识我的。"

她叹了口气,将书放在一边。"你们这些人怎么都这么想,好像我们女孩子是迷路的小动物,随随便便一伸手就能捡到似的。你把我当成什么人了?"

"你顺走了我的钱夹。"他说。他很得意地,他用的是"顺走"这个词,他觉得"顺"比"偷""拿",甚至"掏",听起来措辞更加准确。

"你在说什么呀?"那个女孩说道。

"我知道是你干的——在杂志柜台边。只要你还给我,我们这事就一笔勾销,否则就把你交给警察。"

她仔细打量着他,表情非常严肃。"好吧。"她说着,将她那只黑包拉到膝盖上,手伸进去,掏出了一只钱包。

他从她手里一把接过来。"等一下,"他说,"这不是我的。"

那女孩撒腿就跑,他在后面穷追不舍,真像电影中的场面——周围的人纷纷避开。那女孩飞快地左拐右转,避免发生碰撞。他的喘息声使他想起了自己的年纪——后来听到一个女人的喊叫声从背后传来:

"抓……抓贼!抓住那个男人!"

前面,黑发女人已经转过拐角,消失不见了。与此同时,一个身穿海军陆战队制服的年轻人伸脚一绊。他重重地跌倒在地,膝盖和胳膊肘磕在大厅的地板砖上，但他的手里仍紧紧地攥着那个别人的钱包。

这个钱包是一个女人的，里面装满了钞票和像"萨克""佩克与佩克""洛德与泰勒"这种公司的信用卡。钱包的主人是那个穿皮毛镶边外套的金发女人——他此前曾经看到过的那个黑发小偷女人交谈的金发女人。她也跑得气喘吁吁，跟那个和她一同赶来的警察一样。

"就是他，"金发女人说，"是他偷了我的钱包。"

他突然想到，他甚至无法向警察证实自己的身份。

两个星期之后——他不再那样尴尬和恼怒，家庭律师的报酬已经支付，家里的风波也已经平息——他的钱包在上午送来的邮件中意外地出现了，没有附加任何解释。钱包原封未动，钱一分也没少，所有的证卡都在。尽管松了口气，但他觉得，在自己今后的人生旅途中，他遇到警察就会感到自责，在女人们面前会感到羞愧。

Thief

He is waiting for the airline ticket counter when he first notices the young woman. She has glossy black hair pulled tightly into a knot at the back of her bead—the man imagines it loosed and cascading to the small of her back—and carries over she shoulder of her leather coat a heavy black purse. She wears black boots of soft leather. He struggles to see her face—she is ahead of him in line—but it is not until she has bought her ticket and turns to walk away that he realizes her beauty, which is pale and dark-eyed and full-mouthed, and which quickens his heart beat. She seems aware that he is staring at her and lowers her gaze abruptly.

The airline clerk interrupts. The man gives up looking at the woman—he thinks she may be about twenty-five—and buys a round-trip, coach class ticket to an eastern city.

His flight leaves in an hour. To kill time, the man steps into one of the airport cocktail bars and orders a scotch and water. While he sips it he watches the flow of travelers through the terminal-including a remarkable number, he thinks, of an unattached pretty women dressed in fashion magazine clothes—until he catches sight of the black-haired girl in the leather coat. She is standing near a Travelers Aid counter, deep in conversation with a second girl, a blond in a cloth coat trimmed with gray fur. He wants somehow to attract the brunette's attention, to invite her to have a drink with him before her own flight leaves for wherever she is traveling, but even though he believes for a moment she is looking his way he cannot catch her eye from out of the shadows of the bar. In another instant the two women separate; neither of their direction is toward him. He orders a second scotch and water.

When next he sees her, he is buying a magazine to read during the flight and becomes aware that someone is jostling him. At first he is startled that anyone would be so close as to touch him, but when he sees who it is he musters a smile.

"Busy place." he says.

She looks up at him—is she blushing? —and an odd grimace crosses her mouth and vanishes. She moves away from him and joins the crowds in the terminal.

The man is at the counter with his magazine, but when he reaches into his back pocket for his wallet the pocket is empty. Where could I have lost it? he thinks. His mind begins enumerating the credit cards, the currency, the membership and identification cards; his stomach churns with something very like fear. The girl who was so near to me, he thinks—and all at once he understands that she has picked his pocked.

What is he to do? He still has his ticket, safely tucked inside his suit coat—he reaches into the jacket to feel the envelope, to make sure. He can take the flight, call someone to pick him up at his destination—since he cannot even afford bus fare—conduct his business and fly home. But in the meantime he will have to do something about the lost credit cards—call home, have his wife get the numbers out of the top desk drawer, phone the card companies—so difficult a process, the whole thing suffocating. What shall he do?

First, find a policeman, tell what has happened, describe the young woman, damn her, he thinks, for seeming to be attentive to him, to let herself stand so close to him, to blush prettily when he spoke—and all the time she wanted only to steal from him. And her blush was not shyness but the anxiety of being caught; that was most disturbing of all. Damn deceitful creatures. He will spare the policeman the details—just tell what she has down, what is in the wallet. He grits his teeth. He will probably never see his wallet again.

He is trying to decide if he should save time for talking to a guard near the X-ray machines when he is appalled and elated to see the black-haired girl. She is seated against a front window of the terminal, taxis and private cars moving sluggishly beyond her in the gathering darkness: she seems engrossed in a book. A seat beside her is empty, and the man occupies it.

"I've been looking for you." he says.

She glances at him with no sort of recognition. "I don't know you." she says.

"Sure you do."

She sighs and puts the book aside. "Is this all you characters think about—picking up girls like we were stray animals? What do you think I am?"

"You lifted my wallet." he says. He is pleased to have said "lifted", thinking it sounds more wordly than stole or took or even ripped off.

"I beg your pardon?" the girl says.

"I know you did—at the magazine counter. If you'll just give it back, we can forget the whole thing. If you don't, then I'll hand you over to the police."

She studies him, her face serious. "All right." she says. She pulls the black bag onto her lap, reaches into it and draws out a wallet.

He takes it from her. "Wait a minute," he says, "This isn't mine."

The girl runs, he bolts after her. It is like a scene in a movie—bystanders scattering, the girl zigzagging to avoid collisions, the sound of his own breathing reminding him how old he is—until he hears a woman's voice behind him:

"Stop, thief! Stop that man!"

Ahead of him the brunette disappears around a corner and in the same moment a young man in a marine uniform puts out a foot to trip him up. He falls hard, banging knee and elbow on the tile floor of the terminal, but manages to hang on to the wallet which is not his.

The wallet is a woman's, fat with money and credit cards from places like Sak's and Peck & Peck and Lord & Taylor, and it belongs to the blonde in the fur-trimmed coat—the blonde he has earlier seen in conversation with the criminal brunette. She, too, is breathless, as is the police man with her.

"That's him," the blonde girl says, "He lifted my billfold."

It occurs to the man that he cannot even prove his own identity to the policeman.

Two weeks later—the embarrassment and rage have diminished, the family lawyer has been paid, the confusion in his household has receded—the wallet turns up without explanation in one morning's mail. It is intact, no money is missing, all the cards are in place. Though he is relieved, the man thinks that for the rest of his life he will feel guilty around policemen, and ashamed in the presence of women.

一小时的故事

凯特·萧邦

大家都知道马德拉夫人的心脏有毛病,所以尽量小心翼翼地把她丈夫的死讯告诉她。

是她的姐姐朱赛芬告诉她的,连一句完整的话都没说,暗示得断断续续、遮遮掩掩的。

她丈夫的朋友理查德也在她身边,正是他在报社收到了铁路事故的消息,那上面"死亡者"名单里,布雷特里·马拉德是第一个名字。他一直等到来了第二封电报,证实了,然后就先人一步匆匆赶来报丧,表示他是一个多么周到细致、体贴入微的朋友。

许多女人听到这样的噩耗,一定会手足无措,无法接受事实,她却一下子倒在姐姐的怀里,放声大哭起来。当哀伤的风暴逐渐减弱时,她独自走进自己的房里,不让别人跟着她。

对着打开的窗户,有一把舒适、宽大的扶手椅,她身体上精疲力竭,并且似乎已浸透到她的心灵深处,她颓坐在扶手椅上。

她能看到房前空地上洋溢着新春活力的树梢在轻轻摇曳,空气里充满了雨水的芬芳。

下面街上有个小贩在叫卖,远处依稀传来了什么人的缥缈的歌声。

屋檐下，数不清的麻雀在叽叽喳喳地叫个不停。

对着她的窗口的正西方，相逢又相叠的朵朵行云之间露出一片一片的蓝天。

她坐在那里，头靠着扶手椅背上的软垫，一动也不动，嗓子眼儿里偶尔抽泣一两声，身子抖动一下，就像那哭着哭着睡着了在梦中还在抽泣的小孩。

她依旧年轻，美丽、淡定的脸上的线条，说明了一种自控，甚至是一种力量。可是，这会儿她目光呆呆的，凝视着远方的一片蓝天，那目光看来她不是在沉思，而像是在理智地思考一个悬而未决的决定。

好像什么东西正向她走来，而她也正等着它，心怀恐惧，是什么东西呢？她不知道，太微妙、太难以捉摸了，难以名状。可是她能感觉到，那是从天空上爬出来的，正穿过洋溢在空气中的声音、气味、色彩而向她奔来。

此时，她的胸狂乱地起伏着，她逐渐认出来那正向她逼近、就要占有她的东西。她努力运用意志把它击溃——可是她的意志就像她那白皙纤弱的双手一样软弱无力。

当她放松自己时，从微张的嘴唇间溜出了低低的声音，她一遍又一遍地低声悄语："自由了，自由了，自由了！"然而接下来，她眼神中流露出一副茫然、恐惧的神情。她的目光明亮而热切，她的脉搏加快了，血液循环让她全身感到温暖而放松。

她没有停下来问问自己，是不是有一种邪恶的快感攫住了她，她感觉头脑清醒，意气风发，认为这根本不重要。

她知道，等她见到死者那双生前温柔亲切、现在僵硬地交叉着的双手时，等她见到那张生前从不吝啬对她的爱意、现在灰白的脸庞时，她还是会哭的，不过透过那痛苦的时刻看到，未来的长长的岁月可就完全属于她了，她张开双臂欢迎这岁月的到来。

在未来的岁月里，她不用为任何人而活，她只为自己而活。那时，她不必再盲目地屈从于任何专横的意志。人们总是认为他们有权把个人的意志强加于他人。她突然感到茅塞顿开，无论其动机是善良的还是残酷的，这种做法与犯罪无异。

当然，她是爱过他的——有时候是爱的，但大多数时候是不爱的，那又有什么关系，有了独立的意志——她现在突然认识到这是她身上最强烈的一种冲动，爱情这个未解的谜团又算得了什么呢！

"自由了！身心自由了！"她继续低声说着。

朱赛芬跪在紧闭的门外，嘴唇对着锁孔，苦苦哀求让她进去。"露易丝，开开门！求求你啦，开开门——你这样会得病的，你干什么呢？看在上帝的份儿上，开开门吧！"

"走开，我不会让自己生病。"确实没有：她正透过那扇开着的窗子畅饮那真正的长生不老药呢。

她在纵情地幻想未来的岁月。春日，还有夏日，以及各种各样的日子都将属于自己。她飞快地做了一个祷告，祈祷未来的日子天长地久，仅仅是在昨天，她在想到未来的日子太长时而瑟瑟发抖。

她终于站了起来，在她姐姐一而再再而三的请求下开了门。她眼睛里充满了胜利的狂热，不知不觉间，她的神态举止竟像胜利女神一样了。她紧搂着姐姐的腰，她们一齐下了楼，理查德正站在下面等着她们。

有人在用钥匙开大门，进来的是布雷特里·马拉德。他看上去稍微有点儿旅途的倦容，但泰然自若地提着他的大旅行包和伞，他距离事故甚远，而且不知道出了事故。他站在那儿，大为吃惊地听见了朱赛芬刺耳的尖叫声,看见了理查德正欲急忙挡住他,不让他妻子看见他。

不过,理查德的动作还是太慢了。

医生来了以后,他们说她是死于心脏病——说她是因为极度高兴致死的。

The Story of an Hour

By Kate Chopin

Knowing that Mrs.Mallard was afflicted with a heart trouble, great care was taken to break to her as gently as possible the news of her husband's death.

It was her sister Josephine who told her, in broken sentences, veiled hints that revealed in half concealing.

Her husband's friend Richards was there, too, near her. It was he who had been in the newspaper office when intelligence of the railroad disaster was received, with Brently Maitard's name leading the list of "killed". He had only taken the time to assure himself of its truth by a second telegram, and had hastened to forestall any less careful, less tender friend in bearing the sad message.

She did not hear the story as many women have heard the same, with a paralyzed inability to accept its significance. She wept at once, with sudden, wild abandonment, in her sister's arms. When the storm of grief had spent itself she went away to her room alone. She would have no one follow her.

There stood, facing the open window, a comfortable, roomy armchair. Into this she sank, pressed down by a physical exhaustion that haunted her body and seemed to reach into her soul.

She could see in the open square before her house the tops of trees that were all aquiver with the new spring life. The delicious breath of rain was in the air.

In the street below a peddler was crying his wares. The notes of a distant song which someone was singing reached her faintly, and countless sparrows were twittering in the eaves.

There were patches of blue sky showing here and there through the clouds that had met and piled one above the other in the west facing her window.

She sat with her head thrown back upon the cushion of the chair, quite motionless, except when a sob came up into her throat and shook her, as a child who has cried itself to sleep continues to sob in its dreams.

She was young, with a fair, calm face, whose lines bespoke repression and even a certain strength. But now there was a dull stare in her eyes, whose gaze was fixed away off yonder on one of those patches of blue sky. It was not a glance of reflection, but rather indicated a suspension of intelligent thought.

There was something coming to her and she was waiting for it, fearfully. What was it? She did not know, it was too subtle and elusive to name. But she felt it, creeping out of the sky, reaching toward her through the sounds, the scents, the color that filled the air.

Now her bosom rose and fell tumultuously. She was beginning to recognize this thing that was approaching to possess her, and she was striving to beat it back with her will—as powerless as her two white slender hands would have been.

When she abandoned herself, a little whispered word escaped her slightly parted lips. She said it over and over under her breath. "Free, free, free!" The vacant stare and the look of terror that had followed it went from her eyes. They stayed keen and bright. Her pulses beat fast, and the coursing blood warmed and relaxed every inch of her body.

She did not stop to ask if it were or were not a monstrous Joy that held her. A clear and exalted perception enabled her to dismiss the suggestion as trivial.

She knew that she would weep again when she saw the kind, tender hands folded in death; the face that had never looked save with love upon her, fixed and gray and dead. But she saw beyond that bitter moment along procession of years to come that would belong to her absolutely. And she opened and spread her arms out to them in welcome.

There would be no one to live for her during those coming years, she would live for herself. There would be no powerful will bending hers in that blind persistence with which men and women believe they have a right to impose a private will upon a fellow creature. A kind intention or a cruel intention made the act seem no less a crime as she looked upon it in that brief moment of illumination.

And yet she had loved him—sometimes. Often she had not. What did it matter! What could love, the unsolved mystery, count for in face of this possession of self-assertion which she suddenly recognized as the strongest impulse of her being!

"Free! Body and soul free!" she kept whispering.

Josephine was kneeling before the closed door with her lips to the keyhole, imploring for admission. "Louise, open the door! Beg, open the door—you will make yourself. What are you doing, Louise? For heaven's sake, open the door."

"Go away. I am not making myself." No, she was drinking in a very elixir of life through that open window.

Her fancy was running riot along those days ahead of her. Spring days, and summer days, and all sorts of days that would be her own. She breathed a quick prayer that life might be long. It was only yesterday she had thought with a shudder that life might be long.

She arose at length and opened the door to her sister's importunities. There was a feverish triumph in her eyes, and she carried herself unwittingly like a goddess of Victory. She clasped her sister's waist, and together they descended the stairs. Richards stood waiting for them at the bottom.

Someone was opening the front door with a latchkey. It was Brently Mallard who entered, a little travel-stained, composedly carrying his gripsack and umbrella. He had been far from the scene of accident, and did not know there had been one. He stood amazed at Josephine's piercing cry, at Richards' quick motion to screen him from the view of his wife.

But Richards was too late.

When the doctors came they said she had died of heart disease—of joy that kills.

怎么对待生活

我问自己,怎么对待生活?

我房间里所有的东西都现身说法,给我提供了完整的答案:

天花板答道:要志存高远。

电风扇答道:要沉着冷静。

钟表答道:要珍惜时间。

日历答道:要与时俱进。

钱包答道:要未雨绸缪。

镜子答道:要一日三省。

墙壁答道:要乐于助人。

窗户答道:要拓宽视野。

地板答道:要永远脚踏实地。

楼梯答道:要步步小心。

最有启发性的答案是:

抽水马桶答道:时辰一到,该放则放。

卫生纸答道:每天都会碰到恶心事,要有心理准备。

How to Handle Life

I asked myself how to handle life?

My room gave me all the answers:

Roof said: Aim high.

Fan said: Be cool.

Clock said: Value time.

Calendar said: Be up to date.

Wallet said: Save now for the future.

Mirror said: Always observe yourself.

Wall said: Share other's load.

Window said: Expand the vision.

Floor said: Always be down to earth.

Stairs said: Watch each step you take.

The most inspiring one:

Toilet bowl said: When it's time to let go, just let it go.

And the toilet paper said: Expect shit everyday.

你是什么人，你已经出卖了自己

你是什么人，你已经出卖了自己，
通过你寻求的友谊，
通过你说话的方式，
通过你消磨业余时间的方式，
通过你消费大钱小钱的方式。

你是什么人，你已经出卖了自己，
通过你身上穿的服饰，
通过你承受压力时的意志，
通过引你开怀大笑的事物，
通过你在留声机播放的唱片。

你是什么人，你已经出卖了自己，
通过你走路的样子，
通过你喜欢谈论的话题，
通过你承受失败的方式，
通过你吃东西的样子这样的琐碎小事，
通过你从满满的书架里挑选出的书籍。

通过这些以及更多的方式,
你是什么人,你已经出卖了自己,
所以确实没有丝毫意义,
还要徒劳地继续伪装到底。

You Tell on Yourself

You tell on yourself,

By the friends you seek,

By the very manner in which you speak,

By the way you employ your leisure time,

By the use you make of dollar and dime.

You tell on yourself,

By the things you wear,

By the spirit in which you burdens bear,

By the kind of things at which you laugh,

By the records you play on the phonograph.

You tell on yourself,

By the way you walk,

By the things of which you delight to talk,

By the manner in which you bear defeat,

By so simple a thing as how you eat,

By the books you choose from the well-filled shelf.

In these ways and more,
You tell on yourself,
So there's really no particle of sense
In an effort to keep up false pretense.

心与手

在丹佛车站，一帮旅客涌进开往东部方向的 BM 公司的快车车厢。在一节车厢里坐着一位衣着优雅、容貌美丽出众的年轻女子，身边摆满奢侈用品，一看便知是一位经验丰富的旅行者。在新上车的旅客中走来了两个人：一位英俊漂亮，表情动作都显得果敢而又坦率；另一位则人高马大，穿着邋遢，面色阴沉，行动拖沓。这两个人的手用手铐铐在一起。

两个人穿过车厢过道，唯一空着的座位朝着车尾的方向，还正对着那位迷人的女郎。这两个铐在一起的人就在这张空位子上坐了下来。年轻的女子开始迅速瞄了他们一眼，目光遥远而冷淡。接下来，她容光焕发的脸上浮现出妩媚的笑颜，圆润的双颊也泛起了淡淡的粉红色。接着只见她伸出那戴着灰色手套的手与来客握手。她开口说话的声音听上去甜美、饱满而淡定，让人感到她是一个习惯于对别人说话，也习惯了让人听她说话的人。

她说道："噢，埃斯顿先生，若是你让我先开口的话，那我就必须开口了。怎么，你认不出在西部见过的老朋友了？"

年轻英俊的那位听到她的声音，立刻大吃一惊，显得局促不安起来，然后他立刻恢复了常态，用左手握住了她的手。

"原来是费尔吉德小姐，"他笑着说，"我请求您原谅我不能用另一只手来握手,因为它现在正派用场呢。"

他微微地抬起右手,只见一副闪亮的"手镯"正把他的右手腕和同伴的左手腕扣在一起。年轻姑娘眼中的兴奋神情渐渐地变成一种莫名其妙的恐惧。脸颊上的红晕也消退了。她双唇也不解地微微张开,力图缓解难过的心情。埃斯顿微微一笑,好像是这位小姐的样子使他发笑一样。他刚要开口解释,他的同伴抢先说话了。这位脸色阴沉的人一直用他那锐利机敏的目光含蓄地观察姑娘的表情。

"请允许我说话,小姐。我看得出您和这位警长一定很熟悉,如果您让他到监狱以后替我说几句好话,那我在那里的处境一定会好多了。他正送我去内森维茨监狱,我因伪造罪在那儿被判处七年有期徒刑。"

"哦,"姑娘深深地吸了一口气,脸色又恢复了红晕,"那么这就是你现在做的差事,当个法警!"

"亲爱的费尔吉德小姐,"埃斯顿淡定地说道,"我不得不找个差事来做。钱有翅膀,自己会飞的。你也清楚,在华盛顿得有钱才能和别人一样地生活。我在西部发现赚钱的机会,所以——嗯,当然法警的地位自然比不上大使,但——"

"大使,"姑娘热情洋溢地说道,"再也没来过电话,我也不需要打电话过去。你懂的。你现在既然成了一位勇敢的西部英雄,骑马,打枪,历经千难万险,那么生活也一定和在华盛顿时大不一样。老朋友们都在怀念你。"

姑娘的眼光再次被吸引到了那副亮闪闪的手铐上,她睁大了眼睛。

"请不要担心,小姐,"另外那位来客又说道,"为了不让犯人逃跑,所有的法警都把自己和犯人铐在一起,埃斯顿先生懂行。"

"要过多久我们才能在华盛顿见面?"姑娘问。

"我想不会很快,"埃斯顿回答,"恐怕我像蝴蝶一样逍遥自在的日子已经结束了。"

"我爱西部，"姑娘没头没脑地说着，眼里闪烁着温柔的光芒。她看着车窗外，开始不再矫揉造作，而是坦诚自然地说道："我和妈妈在丹佛度过了整个夏天，因为父亲偶染小恙，她一个星期前回家了。我会在西部过得很快乐，我想这儿的空气适合我。金钱不是万能的，但人们常常对事物产生误解，还一错再错——"

"我说，法警先生，"脸色阴沉的那位大声地喊道，"这太不公平了，我需要喝点什么，我一天没抽烟了。你们聊够了没有？现在带我去抽烟车厢，好吗？我真想过过瘾。"

这两位铐在一起的旅行者站起身来，埃斯顿脸上依旧挂着未退去的微笑。

"我可不能拒绝抽烟的请求，"他轻声说，"烟是不幸者的一个朋友。再见，费尔吉德小姐，工作需要，您能理解。"他伸手来握别。

"你现在去不了东部太遗憾了。"她一面说着，一面重新整理好衣裳，恢复了仪态和风度，"但我想你一定会继续旅行，到内森维茨去吧？"

"是的，"埃斯顿回答，"我必须去内森维茨。"

两位来客侧着身子地穿过车厢过道进了吸烟室。

另外两个坐在附近的旅客几乎一字不漏听到他们的全部谈话，其中一个说道："那位警长真是条好汉，很多西部人都这么厉害。"

"担任一个这么大的职务，年轻有为，是吗？"另一个问道。

"年轻！"第一个人大叫道，"为什么——哦！你真的看准了吗？我是说——你见过把犯人铐在自己右手上的法警吗？"

Hearts and Hands

At Denver there was an crowd of passengers into the coaches on the eastbound B. & M. express. In one coach there sat a very pretty young woman dressed in elegant taste and surrounded by all the luxurious forts of an experienced traveler. Among the newers were two young men, one of handsome presence with a bold, frank face expression and manner; the other a ruffled, glum-faced person, heavily built and roughly dressed. The two were handcuffed together.

As they passed down the aisle of the coach the only available seat offered was a reversed one facing the attractive young woman. Here the linked couple seated themselves. The young woman's glance fell upon them with a distant, swift disinterest; then with a lovely smile brightening her face and a tender pink tingeing her rounded cheeks, she held out a little gray-gloved hand. When she spoke her voice, full, sweet, and deliberate, proclaimed that its owner was accustomed to speak and be heard.

"Well, Mr. Easton, if you will make me speak first, I suppose I must. Don't you ever recognize old friends when you meet them in the West? "

The younger man aroused himself sharply at the sound of her voice, seemed to struggle with a slight embarrassment which he threw off instantly, and then clasped her fingers with his left hand.

"It's Miss Fairchild, " he said, with a smile. "I'll ask you to excuse the other hand; it's otherwise engaged just at present."

He slightly raised his right hand, bound at the wrist by the shining "bracelet" to the left one of his panion. The glad look in the girl's eyes slowly changed to a bewildered horror. The glow faded from her cheeks. Her lips parted in a vague, relaxing distress. Easton, with a little laugh, as if amused, was about to speak again when the other forestalled him. The glum-faced man had been watching the girl's face expression with veiled glances from his keen, shrewd eyes.

"You'll excuse me for speaking, Miss, but, I see you're acquainted with the officer here. If you'll ask him to speak a word for me when we get to the pen he'll do it, and it'll make things easier for me there. He's taking me to Leavenworth prison. It's seven years for cheating."

"Oh!" said the girl, with a deep breath and returning color. "So that is what you are doing out here. An officer!"

"My dear Miss Fairchild, " said Easton, calmly, "I had to do something. Money has a way of taking wings with itself, and you know it takes money to keep step with our crowd in Washington.

I saw this opening in the West, and—well, an officer isn't quite as high a position as that of ambassador, but—"

"The ambassador," said the girl, warmly, "doesn't call any more. I needn't ever have done so. You ought to know that. And so now you are one of these brave Western heroes, and you ride and shoot and go into all kinds of dangers. That's different from the Washington life. You have been missed from the old crowd."

The girl's eyes, fascinated, went back, widening a little, to rest upon the glittering handcuffs.

"Don't worry about them, miss," said the other man. "All officers handcuff themselves to their prisoners to keep them from getting away. Mr. Easton knows his business."

"Will we see you again soon in Washington?" asked the girl.

"Not soon, I think," said Easton. "My butterfly days are over, I fear."

"I love the West," said the girl irrelevantly. Her eyes were shining softly. She looked away out the car window. She began to speak truly and simply without the gloss of style and manner:

"Mamma and I spent the summer in Denver. She went home a week ago because father was slightly ill. I could live and be happy in the West. I think the air here agrees with me. Money isn't everything. But people always misunderstand things and remain stupid—"

"Say, officer," shouted the glum-faced man. "This isn't

quite fair. I'm needing a drink, and I haven't had a smoke all day. Haven't you talked long enough? Take me in the smoker now, won't you? I'm half dead for a pipe."

The bound travelers rose to their feet, Easton with the same slow smile on his face.

"I can't deny a require for tobacco," he said, lightly. "It's the one friend of the unfortunate. Good-bye, Miss Fairchild. Duty calls, you know." He held out his hand for a farewell.

"It's too bad you are not going East," she said, reclothing herself with manner and style. "But you must go on to Leavenworth, I suppose?"

"Yes," said Easton, "I must go on to Leavenworth."

The two men sidled down the aisle into the smoker.

The two passengers in a seat near by had heard most of the conversation. Said one of them: "That officer is a good sort of man. Some of these Western fellows are all right."

"Pretty young to hold an office like that, isn't he?" asked the other.

"Young!" exclaimed the first speaker, "Why—Oh! Didn't you catch on? Say—did you ever know an officer to handcuff a prisoner to his right hand?"

一个简单的建议

丽塔·卢西尔

"我今晚需要见你。"听到电话那头那个急切的声音,我的后脊梁打了个冷战。我交往的这个男人为什么坚持要在一个工作日的晚上开车行驶三十英里来见我,我说不准。我已经工作了一整天了,当天晚上在附近的一个大学教课,我的唯一计划只跟花生酱、果酱和法兰绒衣服有关。可是,他的声音里有一种不可抗拒的东西,于是我套上一条旧牛仔裤和一件毛衣,同意见他。

厄尼到了,看起来忧心忡忡。出事了。我们驱车到附近的运动酒吧时,我的头脑在快速运转。我想,也许他要跟我分手。说到底,我最近已经不太专注了,精力被新工作的要求和儿子的要求消耗了。也许他遇到了别的人,因为他人品好,所以坐下来当面告诉我。

不论是什么原因,有一点再清楚不过了:今晚我就会听到。

当我们麻利地溜进一个小间,要了两杯啤酒,一盘玉米片,我意识到自己企图用喋喋不休来打破沉默。

"那么,凯尔特人呢?"

"你能相信风有这么大吗?"

"汤姆·汉克斯,你一定爱死那个家伙。"

我说的什么话题似乎都不能把他暖过来。

然后，一转眼的工夫，他从口袋里掏出一个小盒子。他小心翼翼地把它放在我面前的桌子上，一句话也没说。我犹豫了一会儿。我环顾四周，在烟雾弥漫的房间里巧妙地放了大量的电视机，电视里的篮球比赛发出嘈杂刺耳的声音。我低头瞥了一眼溅在褪了色的牛仔裤上的萨尔萨酱，不觉莞尔。有时候，生活会在你最意想不到的时候及时接住你。

突然之间，我成了不知道说什么才好的人。我拿起小盒子掀开了盖子，那一刹那就是永恒。

我知道他在等待我说的每一个词，而他只想听到的那个词就是"好的"。可是，我能这么说吗？答应嫁给一个人的承诺可没有那么简单，事实上，当时我生活里的一切似乎都不简单。

例如，给我的房子贷款，房子还是这幢房子，银行还是这家银行。只是比率更划算。但是申请以后，要进行信用检查和重新估价，还有一大堆的文件要签署。一切都不是那么简单。

就连买牙膏，有时似乎令人难以置信得复杂。我想让牙齿变白还是变亮？我应该加氟还是去除牙菌斑？我是要买多数牙医使用的那种呢，还是"大鸟先生"代言的那种牙膏对我而言已足够好了？

在那里，我坐在我余生走向的峭壁边上，和那个可能成为丈夫的人面对面，只要我能说出那三个字母的小词就好了。那么简单。然而，却如此艰难。

对我的沉默感到失望，于是他开车送我回家。那天晚上剩下的时间里，我从各个角度剖析了他求婚这件事。我了解他吗？我是说，我真的了解他吗？和他生活在一起会是什么感觉？他生气时脸会涨红吗？他打鼾吗？我们将来住在哪里？婚姻第一次失败以后，我又怎能相信它呢？我的家人会怎么想？我的朋友会怎么说？最重要的是，我的儿子呢？

对我来说，我年幼的儿子是最大的问题。最近几年，杰夫已经习惯了让我只属于他一个人。他会怎么说？他会有什么感觉？

我从钱包里拿出那个小盒子，给他看戒指。连五岁的孩子，都能对我脸上的怀疑表情一目了然。

"妈妈，你爱他吗？"

"是的。"

"那么你应该嫁给他。"

我儿子迅速地把我带回到了事情的核心。从字面上看，他以一个孩子特有的清晰，提醒我，有些事情其实很简单。根本没有那么复杂：我们成年人有时选择去相信的时候考虑得太复杂。

"你爱他吗？"

在我的复杂世界，我差不多已经忘却了有些事情在本质上是非常浅显的。真的很原始。爱就是如此。倘若你真爱一个人的话，就会一目了然，水到渠成。

正如我在我们这个十年结婚纪念日所写的那样，我不得不说过去是这样，现在也是这样。

A Simple Proposition

By Rita Lussier

"I need to see you tonight." The urgency in the voice on the other end of the phone sent a cold chill curling up my spine. Why the man I was dating insisted on traveling thirty miles to see me on a week night, I wasn't sure. I'd worked all day, taught at a nearby university that evening, and my only plans had to do with peanut butter and jelly and a flannel night gown. But something in his voice was compelling. So I pulled on an old pair of jeans and a sweater and agreed to see him.

Ernie arrived looking worried. Something was up. As we drove in silence to a nearby sports bar, my mind raced. Perhaps, I speculated, he wanted to break off our relationship. After all, I had been less attentive lately, consumed by the demands of my new business and my son. Maybe he had met someone else and was a good enough guy to sit down one-on-one and tell me the news.

Whatever it was, one thing was clear: This was the night I was going to hear about it.

As we slid into a booth, and ordered two beers and a platter of nachos, I found myself chattering to fill the silence.

"So, how about those Celtics?"

"Can you believe how windy it is?"

"Tom Hanks, you gotta love the guy."

Nothing I said seemed to warm him up.

Then, in a flash, he pulled a tiny box from his pocket. He placed it gingerly on the table in front of me without saying a word. For a moment, I hesitated. I looked around. The basketball game blared on the phalanx of television sets strategically placed throughout the smoky room. I glanced down at the salsa I had spilled on my faded jeans and smiled. Sometimes, life catches you when you least expect it.

Suddenly, I was the one who didn't know what to say. I picked up the box and opened the lid. This was it. The moment that could last a lifetime.

I knew he was hanging on my every word. And the only word he wanted to hear was "yes." But how could I say that? The commitment to marry someone isn't that simple. In fact, at that moment, nothing in my life seemed simple.

Refinancing my house, for instance. Same house. Same bank. Just a better rate. But after the application, credit checks and reappraisal, there was still a mountain of documents to sign. All for something that seemed so simple.

Even buying toothpaste, at times, seemed mind-boggling. Did I want to whiten or brighten? Should I add fluoride or remove plaque? Did I want the kind more dentists use or was Big Bird's endorsement good enough for me?

There I sat on the precipitous brink of what could be the rest of my life, face-to-face with the man who could be the one, if only I could say that little, three-letter word. So simple. Yet, so hard.

Disappointed by my silence, he drove me home. For the rest of that night, I dissected his proposal from every angle. Did I know him? I mean, did I really know him? What would it be like to live with him? Did his face turn red when he was angry? Did he snore? Where would we live? How could I trust in marriage again when it had failed me the first time? What would my family think? What would my friends say? Above all, what about my son?

For me, my little boy was the biggest question of all. In recent years, Geoff had grown accustomed to having me all to himself. What would he say? How would he feel?

From my purse, I pulled out the tiny box and showed him the ring. The look of doubt on my face must have been wildly evident even to a five-year-old.

"Mom, do you love him?"

"Yes."

"Then you should marry him."

In one quick exchange, my son had brought me back to the heart of the matter. Literally, with a child's clarity, he reminded me that some things really are quite simple. Not nearly as complicated as we grown-ups sometimes choose to believe.

"Do you love him?"

In my complex world, I had almost forgotten that there are some things in nature that are elemental. Primal, really. Love is like that. If you truly love someone, then all the rest will fall into place.

And as I write this on the occasion of our tenth wedding anniversary, I have to say it did. And it does.

你恰逢其时

纽约的时间比加利福尼亚早 3 个小时,
加利福尼亚的时间却没有纽约慢。
有人 22 岁就毕业了,
却苦等了 5 年才找到好工作!
有人在弱冠之年（25 岁）就出任 CEO,
却在大衍之年（50 岁）早逝。
而有人在大衍之年出任 CEO,
却活到了鲐背之年（90 岁）。
有人还是孑然一身,
有人已经喜结连理。
奥巴马在他 55 岁时退出政坛,
而川普却在古稀之年（70 岁）入主白宫。
这个世界上每个人都绝对是在按照自己的时区成长。
你周围的人有的貌似比你领先,
有的貌似比你落后,
可是,每个人都在跑他们自己的比赛,
每个人都在用他们自己的时间。
无须羡慕妒忌他们,

也无须对他们嗤之以鼻。
他们在他们的时区,
而你在你的时区!
生命就是伺机而动。
所以,放松吧。
你既没迟到,
你也没早到,
你恰逢其时,也正在你的时区。

You Are Very Much on Time

New York is 3 hours ahead of California,
but it does not make California slow.
Someone graduated at the age of 22,
but waited 5 years before securing a good job!
Someone became a CEO at 25,
and died at 50.
While another became a CEO at 50,
and lived to 90 years.
Someone is still single,
while someone else got married.
Obama retires at 55,
but Trump starts at 70.
Absolutely everyone in this world works based on their Time Zone.
People around you might seem to go ahead of you,
some might seem to be behind you.
But everyone is running their own RACE,
in their own TIME.

Don't envy them or mock them.

They are in their TIME ZONE,

and you are in yours.

Life is about waiting for the right moment to act.

So, RELAX.

You're not LATE.

You're not EARLY.

You are very much ON TIME, and in your TIME ZONE Destiny set up for you.

初 雪

亨利·朗费罗

初雪翩然而至。赏心悦目,夜以继日,无声无息,落在高山之巅,落在低洼草原,落在生者的屋顶,落在逝者的坟茔!

天地皆白,唯有河流曲折蜿蜒,为雪景增墨线;枯藤老树,枝丫盘错,为灰色天际添美颜!

雪静安,万籁俱寂,若绝世出尘!

万籁声咽,尘嚣化天籁,声声软。

不闻马蹄嘚嘚,不闻车轮辚辚!唯闻雪橇铃儿响叮当,宛若童心搏动疾且欢。

The First Snow

By Henry Longfellow

The first snow came. How beautiful it was, falling so silently, all day long, all night long, on the mountains, on the meadows, on the roofs of the living, on the graves of the dead!

All white save the river, that marked its course by a winding black line across the landscape, and the leafless trees, that against the leaden sky now revealed more fully the wonderful beauty and intricacy of their branches!

What silence, too, came with the snow, and what seclusion!

Every sound was muffled, every noise changed to something soft and musical.

No more trampling hoofs, no more rattling wheels! Only the chiming of sleigh-bells, beating as swift and merrily as the hearts of children.

仇 恨

亨德里克·威廉·房龙

突然之间，战争结束了，希特勒抓到了，押解到了阿姆斯特丹。军事法庭判他死刑。可怎么个死法？枪毙了吧？上绞刑架吧？都未免死得太快、太便宜了他。后来，不知是谁说出了大家的心里话：此人造成的苦难简直令人难以置信，应该把他烧死。

"可是，"有一名法官不赞成，"我们阿姆斯特丹最大的广场也只能容纳万把人，可他要死了，到时候男男女女、妇女儿童，少说也有700万人啊，是荷兰人谁不想上前去咒他一句。"

于是，又一名法官出了个点子，应该把希特勒绑在火刑架上烧死，不过木柴要拿一把火药来点着，火药用一根长引线来引爆，引线应该从鹿特丹牵起，然后沿着主干公路，走德尔夫特、海牙、莱登、哈勒姆，再接到阿姆斯特丹。这样一来，千家万户百万民众，簇拥在连接这几座城市的宽阔大道上，都可以一睹这根引线由南向北一路燃去，直到把为希特勒阁下举行火葬的柴火堆点着。

对于这样的惩罚是否妥当，还特地举行了一次公民投票。计有4981076票赞成，一票反对。投反对票者提出，应对希特勒处以四马分尸。

这个盛大的日子终于来临了。六月的一天，清晨四点整，葬仪开始。有一位母亲，她的三个儿子都被纳粹杀害了，说是犯有莫须有的破坏行为罪。如今引线就由她来点燃，这时唱诗班唱起了一首庄严的感恩赞美诗。接着人群里爆发出一阵胜利的欢呼。

火花从鹿特丹慢慢燃到德尔夫特，往前再奔阿姆斯特丹的广场。全国各地的人从四面八方涌来。上年纪的、有残疾的、遇害人质的亲属，都设有专门的席位接待。

希特勒身穿黄色长衫，已经被锁链拴在了火刑柱上。他始终自我克制着一声不吭，直到有个小男孩爬上这位元首身边的柴堆，贴上一张告示，写的是："我是世界上最大的刽子手。"这下让希特勒的情绪失控，他居然故态复萌，破口大骂起来。

观众一时都愣住了：这么个小矮子竟然大放厥词，活像是在对他的信徒训话，真是一大奇观，真是荒唐。接着是一片狂吼和嘲笑，把他给镇住了。

最重大的时刻到了，下午三点钟左右，火花燃到了阿姆斯特丹的郊区。顿时鼓声震天。接着，人们怀着从未有过的激动的心情，唱起了国歌《威尔海尔慕斯》。希特勒这时面如死灰，徒劳地在锁链里挣扎。

国歌唱完了，火花离火药只有几英尺了，再过六分钟，希特勒就不得好死了。观众的深仇大恨一下子迸发出来，吼声大作。一分钟过去了，又过了一分钟，再次安静下来。眼看引线只剩下几英寸了。就在这时，却发生了一件不可思议的事情。

有个瘦小干枯的小个子男人，趁执行警戒的那队士兵不注意钻了进去。谁都知道他有过怎样的遭遇：他有两个儿子，被伞兵部队拿机枪扫射死了；他的妻子和三个女儿，都在鹿特丹的大屠杀中丧生。从那时起，这个可怜的人就好像一直神志不清，他漫无目的地到处流浪，全靠社会上的慈善团体养着——一个全世界都同情的人。

可眼下他的举动触犯了众怒,大家脸都气白了,原来他特意跑来踩那根引线,把火踩灭了。

"杀了他!杀了他!"众人叫嚷起来。只见老人面对着杀气腾腾的群众,非常淡定。他缓缓地朝天举起双臂。接着,他咬牙切齿地说道:

"咱们从头再点一次!"

Hate

By Hendrik Willem Van Loon

Suddenly the war was over, and Hitler was captured and brought to Amsterdam. A military tribunal condemned him to death. But how should he die? To shoot or hang him seemed too quick, too merciful. Then someone uttered what was in everybody's mind: the man who had caused such incredible suffering should be burned to death.

"But," objected one judge, "our biggest public square in Amsterdam holds only 10,000 people, and 7,000,000 Dutch men, women and children will want to be there to curse him during his dying moments."

Then another judge had an idea. Hitler should be burned at the stake, but the wood was to be ignited by the explosion of a handful of gunpowder set off by a long fuse which should start in Rotterdam and follow the main road to Amsterdam by way of Delft, The Hague, Leiden and Haarlem. Thus millions of people crowding the wide avenues which connect those cities could watch the fuse burn its way northward to Herr Hitler's funeral pyre.

A plebiscite was taken as to whether this was a fitting punishment. There were 4,981,076 yes and one nay. The nay was voted by a man who preferred that Hitler be pulled to pieces by four horses.

At last the great day came. The ceremony commenced at four o'clock on a June morning. The mother of three sons who had been shot by the Nazis for an act of sabotage they did not commit set fire to the fuse while a choir sang a solemn hymn of gratitude. Then the people burst forth into a shout of triumph.

The spark slowly made its way from Rotterdam to Delft, and on toward the great square in Amsterdam. People had come from every part of the country. Special seats had been provided for the aged and the lame and the relatives of murdered hostages.

Hitler, clad in a long yellow shirt, had been chained to the stake. He preserved a stoical silence until a little boy climbed upon the pile of wood surrounding the former Fuhrer and placed there a placard which read, "This is the world's greatest murderer." This so aggravated Hitler's pent-up feelings that he burst forth into one of his old harangues.

The crowd gaped, for it was a grotesque sight to see this little man ranting away just as if he were addressing his followers. Then a terrific howl of derision silenced him.

Now came the great moment of the day. About three o'clock in the afternoon the spark reached the outskirts of Amsterdam.

Suddenly there was a roll of drums. Then, with an emotion such as they had never experienced before, the people sang the Wilhelmus, the national anthem. Hitler, now ashen-gray, futilely strained at his chins.

When the Wilhelmus came to an end the spark was only a few feet from the gunpowder; five more minutes and Hitler would die a horrible death. The crowd broke forth in a shout of hate. A minute went by. Another minute. Silence returned. Now the fuse had only a few inches to go. And at that moment the incredible happened.

A wizened little man wriggled through the line of soldiers standing guard. Everybody knew who he was. Two of his sons had been machine-gunned to death by parachute troops; his wife and three daughters had perished in Rotterdam's holocaust. Since then, the poor fellow had seemed deprived of reason, wandering aimlessly about and supported by public charity—an object of universal pity.

But what he did now made the crowd turn white with anger. For he deliberately stamped upon the fuse and put it out.

"Kill him! Kill him!" the mob shouted. But the old man quietly faced the menacing populace. Slowly he lifted both arms toward heaven. Then in a voice charged with fury, he said:

"Now let us do it all over again!"

一扇关上的门

凯莉·梅特卡夫

我已经盯着我的手机看了大约两个小时了。电话号码都拨了，我只要按一下通话按钮就行了，但我却没有勇气去按。我的心都要从胸膛里跳出来了。我是多么想打电话给他，告诉他我此时的感受。我想告诉他我多么想继续和他在一起。怎么就这么难呢？我所要做的只是给他打个电话，告诉他我的感受而已，如此而已。如果他对我有同样的感觉也没关系，至少他会了解，而我不用一直问自己"万一呢"。

又过了一个小时，然后又是一个小时，然后又是一个小时。为什么我不能这么做？我照了照镜子里，告诉自己我能做到。我必须给自己勇气。我起身下床，翻了翻我的梳妆台的抽屉里。我发现一张我和杰克坐在沙发上的照片。当我笑着盯着摄像机时，他在我脸颊上轻轻地吻了一下。我的脑海里闪过那个夜晚。我们在他的沙发上用他的照相机拍照打发时间。那天晚上我们都哈哈大笑不止。当我现在想起他时，我都忍不住笑。那个晚上，他告诉我他爱我。

当时，我们已经约会一年了。自从我们大学一年级就邀请我出去以后，我们的关系一直很好。大二那年三月，我收到他发来的短信，说他遇到了别人。他说："我认为如果你继续向前走就最好不过了。"当我读到这个短信的时候，我简直不敢相信自己的眼睛。我顿时感觉百味杂陈。我很生气，他做得非常不得体，居然没有当面告诉我。我很难过，他不再爱我了。我很害怕，没有了他我可怎么办。我回到现实，感到一滴眼泪顺着脸颊流下来。我希望能爬进他温暖的臂膀里，让他抱紧我。我希望他能擦干我的眼泪，告诉我一切都会好起来的。我知道我为他哭泣是在浪费时间。我一直都知道，但我不介意。我就是想把时间浪费在他身上。我不想忘记他。

听到门铃响的时候，我擦去了眼泪。我过去开门，当我打开门的时候，我看到了几个月来给我带来痛苦的那个人的脸。

"嘿，克丽。"他尴尬地说道。我所能做的就是目不转睛地盯着他，微微一笑。"我知道我没有权利来这里说这些，可是我与你分手是我犯的一个大错。我很抱歉。"

我只是站在那里，考虑该说些什么。我抬起头看着他美丽的蓝眼睛，那里缺少了什么。当我看到他时，我并没有感到那种温暖、晕眩的感觉。就在那一刻，我意识到，在过去的四个月里，在痛苦和泪水中，我继续前进了。我改变了。我长大了。我成熟了。不管你怎么描绘吧，我都已经忘记他了。所以，我当时只说了一句话："谢谢你顺路过来，但我想你最好继续往前走。"然后，我对他关上了门。在某种程度上，我也对他关上了我心中的门。我冲回卧室，挂断电话，然后把我们俩的照片永远留在心里。

A Closed Door

By Keri Metcalf

I had been staring at my cell phone for about two hours now. The number was completely dialed and all I had to do was press the talk button, but I couldn't bring myself to do it. My heart was beating out of my chest. I wanted so badly to be able to call him and tell him how I felt. I wanted to tell him how much I wanted to be with him again. Why was this so hard? All I had to do was call him and tell him how I felt. That's it. It didn't matter if he felt the same way about me, at least he would know and I wouldn't keep asking myself "what if".

Another hour passed, and then another, and then another. Why couldn't I just do it? I looked at myself in the mirror and told myself that I could do this. I had to give myself courage. I got up off the bed and rummaged around in a drawer in my dresser. I found a picture of Jake and me sitting on a couch. He was giving me a peck on the cheek while I was laughing and staring at the camera. My mind flashed back to that night. We were goofing around on his couch with his camera. All we did was laugh that night. I couldn't help but smile when I thought of him. That was the night he told me he loved me.

We had been dating for a year at that point. Our relationship had been going great ever since he asked me out during our freshman year. It was March of our sophomore year when I received a text message from him saying that he had met someone else. "I think it's best if you just move on," he had said. I couldn't believe my eyes when I read it. I felt so many emotions all at once. I was angry that he didn't have the decency to tell me to my face, upset that he didn't love me anymore, and scared of what I was going to do without him. I came back to the present and felt a tear roll down my cheek. I wished I could crawl into his warm arms and have him hold me tight. I wished he would dry my tears and tell me everything was going to be okay. I knew I was wasting my time crying over him. I had always known, but I didn't mind. I wanted to waste my time over him. I didn't want to get over him.

I wiped the tears from my eyes when I heard the doorbell ring. I walked to answer the door and when I opened it I saw the face of the person who had caused me pain all these months.

"Hey Keri," he said awkwardly. All I could do was stare at him and give him a slight smile. "I know I have no right to come here and say this, but I made a huge mistake breaking up with you. I'm so sorry."

I just stood there trying to figure out what to say. I looked up into his beautiful blue eyes and something was missing. I wasn't getting that warm, giddy feeling when I saw him. And that was the moment I realized that through all the pain and tears I had suffered through the past four months, I had moved on. I changed. I grew up. I matured. Whatever you want to call it, I had gotten over him. All I said was, "Thanks for stopping by, but I think it's best if you just move on," and then I closed the door on him. In a way, I closed the door on him in my heart as well. I rushed back to my bedroom and hung up my phone and then tucked the picture of the two of us away in my heart forever.

令人脑洞大开的墓志铭

当我年轻的时候，我自由自在，想象力天马行空，无拘无束，我梦想着改变这个世界。

当我年龄渐长、心智成熟以后，我发现我不能够改变这个世界，于是将目光放短浅了些，决定只改变这个国家。然而，这个国家似乎也无法改变。

当我进入暮年以后，我抱着最后一丝希望奋力一搏，决定只去改变离自己最近的家人，可是，天哪，他们却没有丝毫改变。

此时此刻，在我弥留之际，我突然意识到：如果一开始我只去改变我自己，这样一来，我就可以给家人树立一个榜样。而在家人的鼓舞与鼓励下，我倒有可能改变这个国家；然后，谁又能说得上呢？我甚至有可能改变这个世界也未可知。

Epitaph

When I was young and free and my imagination had no limits, I dreamed of changing the world.

As I grew older and wiser, I discovered the world would not change, so I shortened my sights somewhat and decided to change only my country. But it, too, seemed immovable.

As I grew into my twilight years, in one last desperate attempt, I settled for changing only my family, those closest to me, but alas, they would have none of it.

And now, as I lie on my deathbed, I suddenly realize: If I had only changed myself first, then by example I would have changed my family. From their inspiration and encouragement, I would then have been able to better my country, and who knows, I may have even changed the world.

什么属于你

一个男人死了……

他意识到自己死了以后,

他看见了上帝提着一个手提箱走到他身旁。

以下是上帝和这个已经死了的男人之间的对话:

上帝:好吧,孩子,到时间了,该上路啦。

男人:这么快?我还有很多计划没有实现呢……

上帝:我向你致歉,可是该上路啦。

男人:你那个手提箱里装的是什么?

上帝:属于你的所有。

男人:我的所有?你是说我的东西吧?是衣服还是钱?

上帝:那些东西从来就不曾属于过你,衣服和钱属于地球。

男人:是我点点滴滴的回忆吧?

上帝:不是,回忆属于时间。

男人:是我的才能吧?

上帝:不是,才能属于机缘巧合。

男人:是我的朋友和家人吧?

上帝:不是,孩子,你的朋友和家人属于你人生的旅途。

男人:是我的妻子和孩子吧?

上帝：不是，你的妻儿属于你的心。

男人：那一定是我的肉体。

上帝：不，不……你的肉体属于尘埃。

男人：那一定是我的灵魂啦！

上帝：孩子，很遗憾，你又错了，你的灵魂属于我。

男人双目含泪，惊恐万状地一把从上帝手里抢过箱子打开——手提箱竟然是空的！！

他伤心欲绝，一颗颗泪珠从面颊上滚落下来，他问上帝……

男人：我竟然什么都不曾拥有过？

上帝：对，你什么都不曾拥有过。

男人：那么，还有什么是属于我的？

上帝：你生命中的一个个刹那，你活着的每一个刹那都是属于你的。生命只是当下的

一，刹，那。

活在当下。

爱在当下。

享受当下吧。

What Was Mine

A man died...

When he realized it,

he saw God coming closer with a suitcase in his hand.

Dialogue between God and Dead Man:

God: Alright son, it's time to go.

Man: So soon? I had a lot of plans...

God: I am sorry, but it's time to go.

Man: What do you have in that suitcase?

God: Your belongings.

Man: My belongings? You mean my things? Clothes... money?

God: Those things were never yours, they belong to the Earth.

Man: Is it my memories?

God: No. They belong to Time.

Man: Is it my talent?

God: No. They belong to Circumstance.

Man: Is it my friends and family?

God: No, son. They belong to the Path you travelled.

Man: Is it my wife and children?

God: No. they belong to your Heart.

Man: Then it must be my body.

God: No, no...It belongs to Dust.

Man: Then surely it must be my Soul!

God: You are sadly mistaken son. Your Soul belongs to me.

Man with tears in his eyes and full of fear took the suitcase from the God's hand and opened it——

EMPTY!!

With heartbroken and tears down his cheek he asks God…

Man: I never owned anything?

God: That's Right. You never owned anything.

Man: Then? What was mine?

God: Your MOMENTS.Every moment you lived was yours. Life is just a Moment…

LIVE IT.

LOVE IT.

ENJOY IT.

足球大赛

汤姆和他的朋友步行去上班。他们一路上都在谈论一场足球大赛。

"你去看比赛吗?"汤姆的朋友问他。

"去不了,我得上班。"汤姆答道。

"好多人都会待在家里看电视转播,他们不会去上班,他们会谎称自己病了。"他的朋友说。

汤姆在贝茨先生的事务所工作。汤姆一进办公室,就发现有一封信在等着他。他打开了信,只见信是以"亲爱的汤姆"开头的:"我给你寄了张这场足球大赛的票,我因病不能成行,只能在家里看电视转播。你可以拿着我的票去看大赛的现场!"汤姆盯着票,不敢相信这是真的,他手中的就是那场足球大赛的票。

办公室的一个女孩儿问道,"发生了什么事?怎么这么高兴?"

汤姆心中暗想:"不能,我不能告诉任何人。"于是他答道,"不过是一个朋友的来信。"

他又看了看球票,心中暗想:"我一定要去看比赛,一定要去。可是我怎么去呀?怎么才能从办公室脱身?我不能跟贝茨先生说我病了,他会猜出我要做什么。他会猜出我想方设法离开办公室就是为了去现场看这场足球大赛。"

汤姆左思右想,根本没心思工作。后来,到了十二点的时候,他有了主意。他起身出了办公室,步行来到街道另一头的一部公共电话前,给他的妹妹珍打了个电话,"珍,我是汤姆。我想让你往我的事务所打个电话,打给贝茨先生。你就说你是在诊所打的电话,告诉他我妈病了。"

"可这是为什么呀?"他妹妹问道。"我今晚再给你解释,现在我不便多说,我得赶紧回事务所。"说完,他挂断了电话。

下午一点的时候,贝茨先生向他走来。"我要告诉你一个坏消息,汤姆。"他说道,"你母亲病了,医生打来了电话,你一定要去看看她。"

"谢谢你,"汤姆说道。"我现在就去,我会尽快赶回来的。"

他快速离开了事务所,直奔足球场。大赛将于三点钟开始,可是足球场里几乎已座无虚席。汤姆的球票位置很好,他可以站在接近前面的位置。这场足球大赛很精彩,电视台的工作人员也在比赛现场进行现场直播,许多人在家里就可以看到赛场上的一切。

次日清晨,汤姆去上班。他一进事务所,大家都看着他,却没有人跟他说话。接着,贝茨先生走到他跟前。"你母亲的病怎么样了?"他问汤姆。

"哦,她好点儿了,谢谢你。"汤姆答道。

"回家吧,"贝茨先生说道,"不要再来事务所上班了,这是你本星期的工资。"他给了汤姆一些钱就转身离开了。

"回家!"汤姆说道,"可是这是为什么呀?为什么我不能在这儿工作了?"

接着,一个女孩开口说道,"你看看这面墙,墙上有一台电视,贝茨先生昨天下午弄来的,他想让我们都能看到这场足球大赛。"

"你们在这里看的电视直播?"汤姆问道。

"对呀,"那个女孩告诉他。"你的球赛票不错啊,是不是?你恰好在所有人的前面,是不是?"

The Big Match

Tom and his friend were walking to work. They were talking about the big football match.

"Are you going to see the match?" Tom's friend asked him.

"No, I must go to work," said Tom.

"Many people will stay at home," his friend said. "They will see the match on television. They won't go to work. They'll say that they are ill."

Tom worked in the office of Mr. Bates. When Tom got to the office, a letter was waiting for him. He opened it. "Dear Tom," the letter began. "I'm sending you a ticket for the big game. I cannot go to the match because I am ill. I shall see it on television. You can go to the match with my ticket." Tom looked at the ticket. He could not believe that he had it. A ticket for the big match!

One of the girls in the office said, "What happened? Why are you so happy?"

"No," Tom thought, "I won't tell anyone." "It's nothing," he said. "Just a letter from a friend."

He looked at ticket again. "I must go to the match," he thought. "I must. But how can I go? How can get out of the office? I cannot tell Mr. Bates that I'm ill. He will know what I'm doing. He'll know I'm trying to get out of the office and go to the big match."

Tom thought and thought. He could not do any work. Then at twelve o'clock he knew what to do. He stood up and went out of the office. He walked to a telephone at the end of the street. He spoke to his sister, Jean. "Jean, this is Tom," he said, "I want you to make a call to my office. Ask to speak to Mr. Bates. Tell him you are speaking from a doctor's. Tell him that my mother is ill."

"But why?" his sister asked. "I will tell you tonight, I can't talk now. I must go back to the office." He put down the telephone.

At one o'clock Mr. Bates came up to him. "I have bad news for you, Tom." He said, "Your mother is ill. The doctor called. You must go to see her."

"Thank you," Tom said. "I'll go now. I'll come back as soon as I can."

He left the office quickly. He went to the football stadium. The big match did not start until three, but the stadium was nearly full. Tom's ticket was a good one, so he could stand near the front. The football match was a good one. The television people were at the match. People at home could see everything on the football grounds.

The next morning, Tom went to work. When he walked into the office everyone looked at him, but no one speak to him. Then Mr. Bates went up to him. "How is your mother?" he asked Tom.

"Oh, she is a little better, thank you." Tom said.

"Go home," Mr. Bates said, "Don't come to this office again. Here's your week's money." He gave Tom some money and walked away.

"Go home!" Tom said, "But why? Why can't I work here?"

Then one of the girls spoke, "Look at the wall, Tom. There is a television on the wall. Mr. Bates brought it in yesterday afternoon. He wanted us all to see the big match."

"You saw the match on TV here?" Tom said.

"That's right," the girl told him. "You had a good ticket, didn't you? You were right at the front of all people, weren't you?"

蓝宝石项链

珍·格雷斯走进皮特·理查德小店的那天，恰恰是皮特最寂寞的日子。这间小店是从皮特的祖父手里继承下来的。各种古玩杂乱地堆放在店前小小的橱窗里：有内战前人们戴的手镯和纪念品盒，有金戒指、银盒子、翡翠、象牙制品和精美的小雕像等。在这个冬日的下午，一个小孩站在橱窗前，前额贴在橱窗的玻璃上，瞪着大大的眼睛，认真地看着每一件珍品，仿佛在寻找着什么特别的东西。最后，她站直身子，脸上带着满意的神情走进店里。

皮特·理查德的店里很阴暗，里面的摆设比橱窗里的还凌乱。首饰盒、决斗手枪、钟和灯等塞在架子上，熨斗、曼陀林和一些都说不出名字的东西则堆在地上。皮特本人站在柜台的后面，年龄还不到三十岁，却已经满头白发。看着这个没戴手套的小顾客把手放在柜台上，他的神情看起来有些阴冷。

"先生，"她开口说道，"您能把橱窗里那串蓝宝石项链拿给我看看吗？"

皮特把项链摊在掌心给她看，项链在他苍白的手上闪闪发光。

"太完美啦，"孩子说道，几乎是自言自语着，"您能帮我把项链包装得漂亮些吗？"

皮特态度冷淡地审视着，问道，"你想买这个送给谁？"

"送给我大姐,她一直照顾着我。这是妈妈去世后的第一个圣诞节,我想送姐姐一份最棒的圣诞礼物。"

"你有多少钱?"皮特小心翼翼地问道。她连忙解开一块裹着的手帕,把有数的几个便士都倒在柜台上。"我把我所有的钱都拿出来了。"她简单地解释道。

皮特若有所思地看着她。然后,他小心地抽回项链。这时,价格标签露了出来,但只有他能看到,小女孩看不到。怎么跟她说呢?小女孩蓝色眼睛里满是信任,这目光触动他隐隐作痛的旧伤。"你等等,"说着,他转身走到储藏室后面。"你叫什么名字?"他边忙边回头问道。

"我叫珍·格雷斯。"

皮特从储藏室出来,手里拿着一个小盒子,盒子用猩红色的纸包装起来,上面还用一条绿色的丝带打了个结。"给你,"他简略地说道,"路上别弄丢了。"

她高兴地跑出店,还回头对他笑了笑。透过窗户,皮特目送着她远去,心头一阵悲凉。珍·格雷斯的某些东西和她那串项链,勾起了他内心深处无法掩饰的悲伤。这个孩子有着麦黄色的头发,海蓝色的眼睛。要知道,皮特曾爱上一个女孩,她也有着同样的麦黄色头发和海蓝色的眼睛。而那串蓝宝石项链本该是她的。

然而,一个雨夜——一辆卡车在光滑的路面上紧急刹车——碾碎了他的梦中情人。从那以后,皮特形影只地生活,内心痛苦万分。工作时,皮特对顾客细心周到,彬彬有礼。但到了晚上,他似乎一如既往地空虚寂寞。他极力想冲破与日俱增的自怜阴霾。然而,珍·格雷斯的蓝眼睛又唤起了他对已逝挚爱的回忆和隐痛。节日期间,顾客们都兴高采烈的,他却因为痛苦显得畏畏缩缩。在接下来的十天里,店里的生意兴隆，叽叽喳喳的女人蜂拥而入，摆弄着各种饰品，讨价还价。最后一个顾客走出店门时，已经是平安夜了，皮特如释重负地舒了口气。又一年过去了，但对皮特来说，这一夜还很漫长。

门开了，一个金发碧眼的年轻女子急急忙忙地走了进来。不知为什么，皮特觉得她很面熟，但又记不起何时何地见过她。她没说话，从手提包里拿出一个用红纸松散地包着的小盒子，上面还有一个用绿色丝带打的结。她打开盒子，一串闪闪发光的蓝宝石项链立刻映入皮特的眼帘。

"这是在您店里买的吗？"她问道。

皮特抬起头，看着她，轻声说："是的，是从我这儿买的。"

"这些宝石是真的吗？"

"是真的。质地虽不是最好的——却是真的。"

"您还记得把它卖给谁了吗？"

"我卖给了一个叫珍的小姑娘。她想把它作为圣诞节礼物送给她姐姐。"

"这串项链多少钱？"

"价格，"他郑重地告诉她，"一直是商家与顾客之间的秘密。"

"可是珍她只有几便士，怎么买得起这串宝石项链呢？"

"她给出了别人给不出的最高价，"他说，"她已经倾其所有。"

接下来，小店霎时变得寂静无声，皮特望着远处钟声正起的教堂尖塔。听着开始响起的钟声，看着柜台上的小盒子，姑娘眼中的疑问，皮特心中涌动无法形容的新生的感觉——这一切都源于一个小孩的爱。

"您为什么要这么做呢？"

皮特把手中的礼物递给她。

"现在是圣诞节的早晨,"他说,"我想送出点儿礼物,但没什么人可送,这太不幸了。我能送你回家,在你家门口说一声圣诞快乐吗?"

于是,伴着声声钟鸣,在幸福的人群中,皮特和这位还不知道姓名的姑娘走出店门,踏入了给世间带来希望的美好的日子的开端。

A String of Blue Beaks

Pete Richard was the loneliest man in town on the day Jean Grace opened the door of his shop. It's a small shop which had come down to him from his grandfather. The little front window was strewn with a disarray of old fashioned things: bracelets and lockets worn in days before the Civil War, gold rings and silver boxes, images of jade and ivory, porcelain figurines. On this winter's afternoon a child was standing there, her forehead against the glass, earnest and enormous eyes studying each treasure as if she were looking for something quite special. Finally she straightened up with a satisfied air and entered the store.

The shadowy interior of Pete Richard's establishment was even more clutterded than his show window. Shelves were stacked with jewel caskets, dueling pistols, clocks and lamps, and the floor was heaped with irons, mandolins and things hard to find a name for. Behind the counter stood Pete himself, a man not more than thirty but with hair already turning gray. There was a bleak air about him as he looked at the small customer who flattened her ungloved hands on the counter.

"Mister," she began, "would you please let me look at the string of blue beads in the window?"

Pete parted the gleamed brightly against the pallor of his palm as he spread the ornament before her.

"They're just perfect," said the child, entirely to herself, "Will you wrap them up pretty for me, please?"

Pete studied her with a stony air. "Are you buying these for someone?"

"They're for my big sister. She takes care of me. You see, this will be the first Christmas since Mother died. I've been looking for the most wonderful Christmas present for my sister."

"How much money do you have?" asked Pete warily. She had been busily untying the knots in a handkerchief and now she poured out a handful of pennies on the counter. "I emptied my bank." she explained simply.

Pete looked at her thoughtfully. Then he carefully drew back the necklace. The price tag was visible to him but not to her. How could he tell her? The trusting look of her blue eyes smote him like the pain of an old wound. "Just a minute," he said, and turned toward the back of the store. Over his shoulder he called, "What's your name?" he was very busy about something. "Jean Grace."

When Pete returned to where Jean Grace waited, a package lay in his hand, wrapped in scarlet paper and tied with a bow of green. "There you are." he said shortly, "Don't lose it on the way home."

She smiled happily over her shoulder as she ran out the door. Through the window he watched her go, while desolation flooded his thoughts. Something about Jean Grace and her string of heads had stirred him to the depths of a grief that would not stay buried. The child's hair was wheat yellow, her eyes sea blue, and once upon a time, not long before, Pete had been in love with a girl with hair of that same yellow and with eyes just as blue. And the turquoise necklace was to have been hers.

But there had come a rainy night—a truck skidding on a slippery road—and the life was crushed out of his dream. Since then, Pete had lived too much with his grief in solitude. He was politely attentive to customers, but after hours his world seemed irrevocably empty. He was trying to forget in a self-pitying haze that deepened day by day. The blue eyes of Jean Grace jolted him into acute remembrance of what he had lost. the pain of it made him recoil from the exuberance of holiday shoppers. During the next ten days trade was brisk; chattering women swarmed in, fingering trinkets, trying to bargain. When the last customer had gone, late on Christmas Eve, he sighed with relief. It was over for another year. But for Pete the night was not quite over.

The door opened and a young woman hurried in. With an inexplicable start, he realized that she looked familiar, yet he could not remember when or where he had seen her before.

Her hair was golden yellow and her eyes were blue. Without speaking, she drew from her purse a package loosely unwrapped in its red paper, a bowl of green ribbon with it. Presently the string of blue beads lay gleaming again before him.

"Did this come from your shop?" she asked.

Pete raised his eyes to hers and answered softly, "Yes, it did."

"Are the stones real?"

"Yes. Not the finest quality—but real."

"Can you remember who it was you sold them to?"

"She was a small girl. Her name was Jean. She bought them for her older sister's Christmas present."

"How much are they worth?"

"The price," he told her solemnly, "is always a confidential matter between the seller and the customer."

"But Jean has never had more than a few pennies of spending money. How could she pay for them?"

"She paid the biggest price anyone can ever pay," he said, "She gave all she had."

There was a silence then that filled the little curio shop. He saw the faraway steeple, a bell began ringing. The sound of the distant chiming, the little package lying on the counter, the question in the eyes of the girl, and the strange of feeling of renewal struggling unreasonably in the heart of Pete, all had come to be because of the love of a child.

"But why did you do it?"

He held out the gift in his hand.

"It's already Christmas morning," he said. "And it's my misfortune that I have no one to give anything to. Will you let me see you home and wish you a Merry Christmas at your door?"

And so, to the sound of many bells and in the midst of happy people, Pete Richard and a girl whose name he had yet to hear, walked out into the beginning of the great day that brings hope into the world for us all.

学艺的正确打开方式

一个年轻人来到当地的一个著名的珠宝鉴定专家面前，述说了自己要成为珠宝鉴定家的愿望。专家担心年轻人学艺没有耐性，对他爱理不理的。年轻人请求给自己一个机会，最后专家应允了，他对年轻人说："你明天来吧。"

第二天上午，专家把一块玉石放到了小伙子的手里让他捧着，然后就自顾自地开始工作起来，他又是切割，又是称重，又是调整宝石的位置。小伙子静静地坐着，等待着。

第三天早晨，专家又把宝石放到小伙子的手里让他捧着。第三天、第四天、第五天，专家的做法和指令都跟第一天一模一样。

第六天，年轻人还是捧着宝石，却再也无法这样继续沉默下去，"师傅，"他问道，"我什么时候才能开始学点手艺啊？"

"你会学的。"专家答道，随后继续做他的事了。

又过了几天，年轻人越来越灰心丧气了。一天上午，专家又走过来让他伸出手来，他正要说再也不想干了，就在话要出口的那一刹那，师傅把宝石放到年轻人手里，而年轻人看都没看手里的宝石，就脱口大叫道："这不是原来那块宝石！"

"你已经开始学手艺了。"师傅说道。

Patience to Learn

A young man presented himself to the local expert on gems and said he wanted to become a gemologist. The expert brushed him off because he feared that the youth would not have the patience to learn. The young man pleaded for a chance. Finally the expert consented and told the youth, "Be here tomorrow."

The next morning the expert put a jade stone in the boy's hand and told him to hold it. The expert then went about his work, cutting, weighing, and setting gems. The boy sat quietly and waited.

The following morning the expert again placed the jade stone in the youth's hand and told him to hold it. On the third, fourth, and fifth day the expert repeated the exercise and the instructions.

On the sixth day the youth held the jade stone, but could no longer stand the silence. "Master," he asked, "when am I going to learn something?"

"You'll learn." the expert replied and went about his business.

Several more days went by and the youth's frustration mounted.

One morning as the expert approached and beckoned for him to hold out his hand, he was about to blurt out that he could go on no longer. But as the master placed the stone in the youth's hand, the young man exclaimed without looking at his hand, "This is not the same jade stone!"

"You have begun to learn." said the master.

致讨厌我的人的一封信

亲爱的讨厌我的人:

感谢你们一直以来臧否我,一直企图搞垮我。感谢你们嘲笑我的每一次失败,感谢你们在学校,我想还有在整个生活里,小人得志时那副得意忘形的样子。感谢你们到处散布关于我的种种飞短流长。

是的,你们挺了解我,但了解得还不够。你们看不到失败和逆境只会让我力量倍增。相应地,当我胜过你们,得到你们不肯给的,然而却是更高层次的承认时,看到你们脸上那目瞪口呆的表情,我也会感到兴奋。你们对我的期待值那么低,这使我可以轻而易举地不断给你们送惊喜。

然而,在大多数情况下,我对自己的现状心满意足,因为你们显然把我视为一种威胁。否则,你们就不会这么讨厌我。你们对我发自肺腑的讨厌只能充当一个指针,证明我所做的是正确的。

正如碧昂斯所说的那样:讨厌我的人,我爱你们,而且我会因为你们所有的人,继续朝着"完美"的方向努力。再重申一遍,感谢你们所做的一切。一定要对我恨恨恨不完哦!

真诚的我

To Haters

Dear Haters,

　Thank you for always devaluing me and always trying to bring me down. Thank you for laughing at all of my failures and being filled with pride when you outshine me in school and, I guess, life in general. Thank you for spreading all gossip that there is about me.

　Yeah, you can read me well but not well enough. You fail to see that failure and adversity only empower me. In return, I receive a thrill when I see the look of surprise on your face when I outshine you and get the higher recognition which you refuse to give me. Your low expectations of me make it pretty easy to continue surprising you.

　For the most part though, I am pretty satisfied with who I am because it is obvious that you see me as a threat. Otherwise, you wouldn't hate me so much. Your genuine hatred towards me only serves as an indicator that I am doing something right.

　Like Beyoncé, I love all of you, my haters, and I will keep on working towards being "flawless" due to you all. Once again, thanks for all that you do. Never stop hating.

Sincerely,
Me

机 票

那天,我当时正在机场,准备买一张去华盛顿的机票,售票员却说,"对不起,我不能卖给你票,我们的电脑崩溃了。"

"你说电脑崩溃了是什么意思?它抑郁了?"

"不,不是抑郁了,所以才崩溃了。"

"也就是说你的电脑一崩溃,就不能给我出票了。"

"是的,我不能给你手写机票吧?机场上唯一允许出票的就是电脑。"

我低头看了看柜台里面,发现空乘都在盯着一个没图像的屏幕喝咖啡。

"那你们这些人都做什么?"

"我们给电脑提供你们的旅程信息,电脑告诉我们你们是否能跟我们一起飞。"

"也就是说只要电脑一崩溃,你们也跟着崩溃了。"

"说得非常好,先生,我以前还没听到有人这么诠释过。"

"电脑一般会崩溃多长时间?"我很想知道。

"我不知道。有时崩溃十分钟,有时崩溃两个小时,不问电脑我们就无从知晓,而电脑既然已经崩溃了,所以也就无法告诉我们。"

"当主要电脑崩溃以后,你们就没有一台备用电脑可以启用吗?"

"恐怕没有。你知道这种机器售价多高吗？"

"我们不谈电脑啦。你们的飞机怎么样了？还能飞吧？"

"不问电脑我就无法告知你，就像我刚才已经告诉你的那样……"

"我知道了，电脑崩溃了。大概我应该去登机口问飞行员他是否会飞华盛顿。"我建议道。

"我都不知道该让你去哪个登机口。"

"我挨个儿试个遍。"

"就算那个飞行员是飞往华盛顿的，你没有机票，他也不可能带你飞。"

"我把机票钱给你，你给我打个收条，这样我就能证明给飞行员看，说我付过款了，好不好？"

"我们不知道怎么收款。电脑每隔一小时更新一次，电脑也是可以收费的唯一历史凭证。"

"我用信用卡怎么样？"

"那就更不行了。电脑一崩溃，就无法识别信用卡给机票的缴费情况了。"

"未来几小时可有飞往华盛顿的其他航班？"

"我不知道，"他说着，手指着电脑的黑屏。"只有它才知道。"

"此时此刻它什么都不知道。"

"它知道还是知道的，"他还要护短，"只是无法告诉我。"

此时，已经有几个人在排队了。"电脑崩溃了"这句话很快就在这几个旅客中传开了，没人知道这句话的确切含义，但是，一些人的脸变得煞白，一些人哭了起来，一些人在踢行李。

一个穿红色夹克衫的男人走了过来，说道，"请大家不要激动，威奇托已经被调查了。"

"威奇托跟这有什么关系？"我问道。

"我们在威奇托的主机崩溃了，不过，只要故障一排除，它就会给每一位误机的旅客买一份免费饮料。"

The Ticket

The other day I was at the airport attempting to buy a ticket to Washington and the attendant said, "I'm sorry, I can't sell you a ticket. Our computer is down."

"What do you mean your computer is down? Is it depressed?"

"No, it can't be depressed. That's why it's down."

"So if your computer is down, just write out me a ticket."

"I can't write you out a ticket. The computer is the only one allowed to issue tickets on the plane."

I looked down the counter and every passenger agent was just standing there drinking coffee and staring into a blank screen.

"What do you all people do?"

"We give the computer the information about your trip, and then it tells us whether you can fly with us or not."

"So when it goes down, you go down with it."

"That's very good, sir. I haven't heard it put that way before."

"How long will the computer be down?" I wanted to know.

"I have no idea. Sometimes it's down for ten minutes. Sometimes for two hours. There is no way we can find out without asking the computer, and since it's down it won't answer us."

"Don't you have a backup computer, when the main computer goes down?"

"I doubt it. Do you know what one of these things costs?"

"Let's forget the computer. What about your planes? They are still flying, aren't they?"

"I couldn't tell without asking the computer, and as I told you…"

"I know. It's down. Maybe I could just go to the gate and ask the pilot if he's flying to Washington," I suggested.

"I wouldn't know what gate to send you to."

"I'll try them all." I said.

"Even if the pilot was going to Washington, he couldn't take you if you didn't have a ticket."

"Why don't I give you money and you could give me a receipt and I could show that to the pilot as proof that I paid?"

"We wouldn't know how to charge. The computer was the only one who keeps track of air fares because they change every hour."

"How about my credit card?"

"That's even worse. When our computer is down it can't notify the credit-card computer to charge the fare to your account."

"Is there any other airline flying to Washington within the next few hours?"

"I wouldn't know," he said, pointing at the dark screen. "Only 'IT' knows."

"And at the moment 'IT' doesn't know anything."

"'IT' knows it," he said defensively, "'IT' just can't tell me."

By this time there were a few people standing in lines. The word soon spread to other travelers that "the computer is down". Nobody knew exactly what this meant, but some people went white, some people started to cry and still others kicked their luggage.

A man in a red jacket came out saying, "Please don't get excited. Wichita has been notified."

"What's Wichita got to do with it?" I asked.

"That's where our main computer went down. But as soon as it gets over its trouble, it's going to buy everyone who missed his plane a free drink."

爱情信使

眼下这个季节和这个时刻，公园里基本没什么游人；那位坐在人行道旁边一条长椅上的年轻女士可能只是一时心血来潮想坐一会儿，提前享受一下即将到来的春天。

她纹丝不动地坐在那里，陷入了沉思。她脸上的那一丝忧伤是近来新添的，因为它尚未改变她青春美丽的面颊，也没柔和她嘴唇上那翘起的果决曲线。

她坐的地方附近有一条小路，一个身材高挑的小伙子正沿着这小路大步穿过公园，他身后跟着个提手提箱的小男童。看到这位年轻的女士，小伙子的脸先是一红，而后又变白了。他越走越近，认真地观察着她脸上的表情，自己的脸上也交织着希望和焦虑。他在距她几码的地方经过，却没有看到任何迹象表明她意识到他来了或他存在。

他又往前走了五十来码，突然停了下来，坐在了路边的长椅上。小男孩放下手提箱，一双机灵的大眼睛盯着他看，大惑不解。年轻人掏出手帕擦了擦额头。手帕精致，小伙子剑眉星目，相貌英俊。他对小男童说道：

"我要你捎个口信给坐在那张长椅的年轻女士，告诉她，我现在要去火车站准备去旧金山，然后去阿拉斯加参加狩猎队打麋鹿。告诉她，既然她不让我和她说话，也不让我给她写信，我也只好用这种方式对她提出最后的请求，请她看在往日的分儿上对我公平些。告诉她，不说明理由，也不让解释，就责备和抛弃一个不该被冤枉的人，我相信这不是她的本性。告诉她，我这样做虽然在某种程度上违背了她的禁令，但我希望她以后能稍稍对我公平点儿。去吧，告诉她这些。"

年轻人往小男童的手里搁了半元银币。小男童肮脏而聪明的脸上一双明亮机灵的眼睛看了他一会儿，随即一溜烟儿跑了过去。他向长椅上的女士跑去，有一点点迟疑却很自然，举起手来碰碰后脑勺上的方格呢的自行车帽檐。那位女士不动声色地看着他，既不冷淡，也不热情。

"女士，"小男童说道，"那张长椅上的先生派我给你表演一段歌舞。要是你不认识那个家伙，他又存心不良的话，你只要说句话，我三分钟之内就找个警察来。要是你认识他，他又是正经人的话，我就把他让我捎的一番话告诉你。"

年轻的女士流露出一丝兴趣。

"一段歌舞表演！"她说道，淡定而甜美的嗓音似乎给她难以捉摸的带有讽刺意味的话语罩上一层若有若无的透明外衣。"这主意倒挺别致——我想他是从民谣歌手那儿学来的吧。我——以前倒是认识派你来的那位先生，所以我想没有什么必要叫警察。你可以表演你的歌舞，不过小点儿声唱，现在演露天歌舞剧早了点儿，那样的话，我们会招来人的。"

"好嘞，"小男童耸了耸肩说，"你知道我的意思，女士。我不是要表演什么，而是说几句话。他让我告诉你，他把衣服都收拾进手提箱，马上要坐车去旧金山了。然后他要去克朗代克打雪鸟。他说你让他别再给你送情书，也别在你花园门前转悠，他就用这种方式点醒你。他说你把他当旧爱判出局，还不给机会对你的决定提出申诉。他说你踹了他,却没解释过原因。"

年轻女士眼神里的那点儿兴趣还在。那个大胆的捕猎鸦的人居然别出心裁,避开了她下达的不准采用常规通讯方式的命令。她凝视着凌乱的公园里矗立的一座孤零零的塑像,对传话人说:

"你去告诉那位先生,我无须再次对他重复表达我的理想,他知道我以前有什么理想,而我现在的理想依然如旧。对于这件事而言,首要的是忠贞不贰和真诚可信。请你告诉他,我已尽最大努力剖析自己,我知道自己的心灵深处需要什么,但更清楚它有软弱的一面。这就是我不让他解释的原因。我指责他的依据不是道听途说,证据充足。不过,既然他坚持要听他已经心知肚明的话,你可以把这个转告给他。

"请你告诉他,那天晚上,我从后面走进花房,去给我母亲折一朵玫瑰花。我亲眼看见他和阿什伯顿小姐在粉红色的夹竹桃底下。那画面太美,可是那亲热的动作本身却太有说服力,是一目了然、不言自明的证据。我离开了花房,同时也丢弃了玫瑰花和我的理想。你把我的这段歌舞带给那位乐团经理吧。"

"实在不好意思,小姐,亲……热,给我解释一下,好吗?"

"亲热——你就说最亲密的接触——要不,你就说太亲密,让人无法保持理想的状态吧。"

小男童又一溜烟儿地跑开了,沙砾在他的脚下飞溅开来,不一会儿到了另一张长椅旁边了。小伙子如饥似渴地投来询问的目光。小男孩作为翻译者,怀着不受个人感情影响的热忱,因而他的双眼闪闪发光。

"小姐说她懂得,当——当小伙子鬼话连篇地乞求和解时,姑娘们最容易上当受骗,所以她拒绝听那些甜言蜜语。她说她亲眼看见你在暖房里跟——一个姑娘又搂又抱,拼命地和那姑娘腻歪。她看来实在恶心。她说你最好还是赶紧赶你的火车去吧。"

听罢信使的话，小伙子低声吹了个口哨，眼睛一亮，突然有了主意。他迅速地将手伸进大衣里边的口袋，掏出了一沓信，从中挑了一封递给小男童，随后又从背心口袋里掏出一块银币给了他。

"把这封信给那位女士送去，"他说道，"请她看一看。告诉她这会让真相大白。告诉她，要是她早在自己理想的信念中掺进一点点对别人的信任的话，自己就不至于这么伤心了。告诉她，她所珍视的忠诚从来没有动摇过。告诉她我在等一个回答。"

信使又站在姑娘的面前了。

"那——那位先生说，你的那些想当然的说法真让他受了委屈。他说他不是那种花花公子，女士，请你看看这——这——封信吧。我敢打赌，他是个清白的人，决不会错。"

亲爱的阿诺德医生：

　　上星期五晚上，我女儿参加沃尔德伦夫人家的宴会时，心脏旧病复发，差点儿晕倒在她家的花房里，当时若不是您在旁扶住了她，妥善照料，我们也许就失去她了。感谢您的善意和及时援手。倘若您能来访并对她进行治疗的话，我会非常高兴。

　　　　　　　　　　　感激您的罗伯特·阿什伯顿

那位年轻的女士把信折了起来，递给了小男童。

"那位先生要你的回答呢。"小信使说道。"说什么？"

女士的目光突然转向了他，眼神明亮，带着笑意，闪着泪光。

"请你告诉那边椅子上的先生，"她笑道，声音发颤，带着幸福，"他的恋人现在就要他过来。"

By Courier

It was neither the season nor the hour when the Park had frequenters; and it is likely that the young lady, who was seated on one of the benches at the side of the walk, had merely obeyed a sudden impulse to sit for a while and enjoy a foretaste of coming Spring.

She rested there, pensive and still. A certain melancholy that touched her countenance must have been of recent birth, for it had not yet altered the fine and youthful contours of her cheek, nor subdued the arch though resolute curve of her lips.

A tall young man came striding through the park along the path near which she sat. Behind him tagged a boy carrying a suit-case. At sight of the young lady, the man's face changed to red and back to pale again. He watched her countenance as he drew nearer, with hope and anxiety mingled on his own. He passed within a few yards of her, but he saw no evidence that she was aware of his presence or existence.

Some fifty yards further on he suddenly stopped and sat on a bench at one side. The boy dropped the suit-case and stared at him with wondering, shrewd eyes. The young man took out his handkerchief and wiped his brow. It was a good handkerchief, a good brow, and the young man was good to look at. He said to the boy:

"I want you to take a message to that young lady on that bench. Tell her I am on my way to the station, to leave for San Francisco, where I shall join that Alaska moose-hunting expedition. Tell her that, since she has commanded me neither to speak nor to write to her, I take this means of making one last appeal to her sense of justice, for the sake of what has been. Tell her that to condemn and discard one who has not deserved such treatment, without giving him her reasons or a chance to explain is contrary to her nature as I believe it to be. Tell her that I have thus, to a certain degree, disobeyed her injunctions, in the hope that she may yet be inclined to see justice done. Go, and tell her."

The young man dropped a half-dollar into the boy's hand. The boy looked at him for a moment with bright, canny eyes out of a dirty, intelligent face, and then set off at a run. He approached the lady on the bench a little doubtfully, but unembarrassed. He touched the brim of the old plaid bicycle cap perched on the back of his head. The lady looked at him coolly, without prejudice or favour.

"Lady," he said, "dat gent on de oder bench sent yer a song

and dance by me. If yer don't know de guy, and he's trying to do de Johnny act, say de word, and I'll call a cop in t'ree minutes. If yer does know him, and he's on de square, w'y I'll spiel yer de bunch of hot air he sent yer." ①

The young lady betrayed a faint interest.

"A song and dance!" she said, in a deliberate sweet voice that seemed to clothe her words in a diaphanous garment of impalpable irony. "A new idea in the troubadour line, I suppose. I used to know the gentleman who sent you, so I think it will hardly be necessary to call the police. You may execute your song and dance, but do not sing too loudly. It is a little early yet for open-air vaudeville, and we might attract attention."

"Awe," said the boy, with a shrug down the length of him, "yer know what I mean, lady. Tain't a turn, it's wind. He told me to tell yer he's got his collars and cuffs in dat grip for a scoot clean out to Frisco. Den he's goin' to shoot snow-birds in de Klondike. He says yer told him not to send 'round no more pink notes nor come hangin' over de garden gate, and he takes dis means of puttin' yer wise. He says yer refereed him out like a has-been, and never give him no chance to kick at de decision. He says yer swiped him, and never said why."

The slightly awakened interest in the young lady's eyes did not

---

① 因为小男孩是个没受过多少教育的孩子，说话多语病，表现为拼写错误。——编者注

abate. Perhaps it was caused by either the originality or the audacity of the snow-bird hunter, in thus circumventing her express commands against the ordinary modes of communication. She fixed her eye on a statue standing disconsolate in the dishevelled park, and spoke into the transmitter:

"Tell the gentleman that I need not repeat to him a description of my ideals. He knows what they have been and what they still are. So far as they touch on this case, absolute loyalty and truth are the ones paramount. Tell him that I have studied my own heart as well as one can, and I know its weakness as well as I do its needs. That is why I decline to hear his pleas, whatever they may be. I did not condemn him through hearsay or doubtful evidence, and that is why I made no charge. But, since he persists in hearing what he already well knows, you may convey the matter.

"Tell him that I entered the conservatory that evening from the rear, to cut a rose for my mother. Tell him I saw him and Miss Ashburton beneath the pink oleander. The tableau was pretty, but the pose and juxtaposition were too eloquent and evident to require explanation. I left the conservatory, and, at the same time, the rose and my ideal. You may carry that song and dance to your impresario."

"I'm shy on one word, lady. Jux—jux—put me wise on dat, will yer?"

"Juxtaposition—or you may call it propinquity—or, if you

like, being rather too near for one maintaining the position of an ideal."

The gravel spun from beneath the boy's feet. He stood by the other bench. The man's eyes interrogated him, hungrily. The boy's were shining with the impersonal zeal of the translator.

"De lady says dat she's on to de fact dat gals is dead easy when a feller comes spielin' ghost stories and tryin' to make up, and dat's why she won't listen to no soft-soap. She says she caught yer dead to rights, huggin'a bunch o'calico in de hot-house. She side-stepped in to pull some posies and yer was squeezin' de oder gal to beat de band. She says it looked cute, all right all right, but it made her sick. She says yer better git busy, and make a sneak for de train."

The young man gave a low whistle and his eyes flashed with a sudden thought. His hand flew to the inside pocket of his coat, and drew out a handful of letters. Selecting one, he handed it to the boy, following it with a silver dollar from his vest-pocket.

"Give that letter to the lady," he said, "and ask her to read it. Tell her that it should explain the situation. Tell her that, if she had mingled a little trust with her conception of the ideal, much heartache might have been avoided. Tell her that the loyalty she prizes so much has never wavered. Tell her I am waiting for an answer."

The messenger stood before the lady.

"De gent says he's had de ski-bunk put on him widout no cause. He says he's no bum guy; and, lady, yer read dat letter, and I'll bet yer he's a white sport, all right."

The young lady unfolded the letter; somewhat doubtfully, and read it.

Dear Dr. Arnold:

I want to thank you for your most kind and opportune aid to my daughter last Friday evening, when she was overcome by an attack of her old heart-trouble in the conservatory at Mrs. Waldron's reception. Had you not been near to catch her as she fell and to render proper attention, we might have lost her. I would be glad if you would call and undertake the treatment of her case.

Gratefully yours, Robert Ashburton

The young lady refolded the letter, and handed it to the boy.

"De gent wants an answer," said the messenger. "Wot's de word?"

The lady's eyes suddenly flashed on him, bright, smiling and wet.

"Tell that guy on the other bench," she said, with a happy, tremulous laugh, "that his girl wants him."

爱与喜欢

面对心爱的人,你心跳如捣;然而,面对你喜欢的人,你心生欢喜。

面对心爱的人,寒冬仿佛暖春;然而,面对喜欢的人,寒冬还是寒冬,只是平添了美丽。

当你凝望心爱的人的双眸时,你会绯红了脸;然而,当你凝望喜欢的人的双眸时,你会嫣然一笑。

面对心爱的人,你纵有千言万语口却难开;然而,面对喜欢的人,你畅所欲言,言无不尽。

面对心爱的人,你会羞羞答答;然而,面对喜欢的人,你会展示真我。

你无法直视心爱的人的双眼;然而,你总能在直视喜欢的人的双眼时嫣然一笑。

当你爱的人潸然泪下的时候,你与他一起痛哭失声;然而,当你喜欢的人潸然泪下的时候,到头来你只是连声劝慰。

爱的感觉始于眼睛;然而,喜欢的感觉却从耳朵开始。

所以,倘若你不再喜欢一个人,你只需堵住双耳就可以一了百了。然而,当你试图闭上双眼的时候,爱,却会化作一颗泪滴,从此永远地留在了你的心底。

Love and Like

In front of the person you love, your heart beats faster, but in front of the person you like, you get happy.

In front of the person you love, winter seems like spring, but in front of the person you like, winter is just beautiful winter.

If you look into the eyes of the one you love, you blush, but if you look into the eyes of the person you like, you smile.

If front of the person you love, you can't say everything on your mind, but in front of the person you like, you can.

In front of the person you love, you tend to get shy, but in front of the person you like, you can show your own self.

You can't look straight into the eyes of the one you love, but you can always smile into the eyes of the one you like.

When the one you love is crying, you cry with him, but when the one you like is crying, you end up comforting.

The feeling of love starts from the eye, and the feeling of like starts from the ears.

So if you stop liking a person you used to like, all you need to do is cover your ears. But if you try to close your eyes, love turns into a teardrop and remains in your heart forever after.

在路上

不论你身在何方,不论你是何方神圣,此刻,以及人生中的每一刻,你我之间有一点恰恰毫无二致,那就是:

我们并非静止不动,而是在路上。

我们的人生是一种运动,一种朝着某个看不见的目的持续稳步、无休无止地行进。

对于我们来说,得失日日有。

即便我们的地位和性格看起来依然如故,其实它们却一直在改变,因为单单时间的流逝就堪称是一种改变。

那块空旷的田野还是那块空旷的田野,一月所见的与七月所见的竟大相径庭。

这是季节变化之功。

同理,孩子身上的天真烂漫在大人身上却不免成了幼稚无能。

我们的每一个所作所为都是朝甲方向或乙方向跨出的一步。

即使失败,本身亦是一种作为。

它引领着我们,不进则退。

We Are on a Journey

Wherever you are and you may be, there is one thing in which you and me are just alike at this moment, and in all the moments of our existence.

We are not at rest, we are on a journey.

Our life is a movement a tendency, a steady, ceaseless progress towards an unseen goal.

We are gaining something, or losing something, every day.

Even when our position and our character seem to remain precisely the same, they are changing, for the mere advance of time is a change.

It is not the same thing to have a bare field in January and in July.

The season makes the difference.

The limitations that are childlike in the child are childish in the man.

Everything that we do is a step in one direction or another.

Even the failure to do something is in itself a deed.

It sets us forward or backward.

时间是什么

时间是什么?

对农民来说,时间就是粮食。

对工人来说,时间就是财富。

对医生来说,时间就是生命。

对士兵来说,时间就是胜利。

对学生来说,时间就是知识。

对科学家来说,时间就是速度。

对企业家来说,时间就是金钱。

对我们大家来说,时间就是一切。

因此,抓住当下吧!

What Is Time

What is Time?

Time is grain for peasants.

Time is wealth for workers.

Time is life for doctors.

Time is victory for soldiers.

Time is knowledge for students.

Time is speed for scientists.

Time is money for businessmen.

Time is everything for all of us.

Therefore, seize the time of today!

半英里

T.O. 比奇克罗夫特

星期六,正午时分。远处市政厅时钟的报时声沉重地响了起来。全城每条街道上的陶瓷厂里汽笛声此起彼伏。男男女女——有成年的,也有未成年的,从二十家陶瓷厂的大门口,鱼贯而出。开始还是三三两两的,很快就形成了一股稳定的人流,然后又三三两两地消失了。

安德鲁·威廉姆森是皇家乔力陶瓷厂的一名浸涂工,他在大门口被守门人琼斯给拦住了。

他说道:"再见,安德鲁,祝你跑半英里交好运。"

安德鲁扫了他一眼,目光不自在地移开了。

"你怎么知道我要跑半英里比赛呢?"

琼斯解释道:"哦,我对这种比赛有兴趣,我以前也跑过半英里比赛。"

安德鲁追问道:"说下去,可我怎么从来没听说过呢?"

老人答道:"我跑过一分五十八秒的好成绩,这在过去算是不错的成绩了。"

"然后呢?"安德鲁继续追问道,"那可是高级赛跑比赛,高级半英里比赛。"

"哦，我不知道，现在不少人都能取得这样的成绩。"

"哎呀，我真希望我能取得这样的成绩，我的理想是：挺进两分钟，到现在为止，我还从来没有突破过两分四秒呐！"

"喔，这只是个时间问题。"老手给他打气，"先在附近好好慢跑热热身，吸点夏天的新鲜空气，你就赢定了。"

"可我从来没参加过高级赛跑啊。"安德鲁还是忧心忡忡。"我只参加过俱乐部组织的赛跑，我不敢奢望取名次拿奖，你也看看参赛的选手啊。"

"都有谁？"琼斯问道。

"嗯，决赛有六个人，咱们一个一个地说：乔·布鲁斯特，是个越野选手，他一英里能跑四分三十秒，现在他想跑半英里。"

"哦，他绝不会超过两分钟，"琼斯斩钉截铁地断言，"我敢担保。"

"还有佩里，他参加上个星期'三个俱乐部'合办的德比大赛，跑了二分四秒。"

"嗯，还有谁？"

"还有雷德布鲁克，是剑桥大学校队的，我根本就没机会。"

"他是个优秀的赛跑选手，"琼斯评论道，"可是，你觉得他在五月训练过吗？不大可能。这可能是他第一次跑，就像测试似的。你训练过吗？"

"认真训练过，"安德鲁说道，"这个月每天晚上都训练，上周参加了一个比赛，成绩还不错。"

"听我的，"琼斯一字一顿地对他说道，"紧紧咬着布鲁斯特。他会在快到四百四十码的时候领跑。你只要盯着他就行，别人不用管。不要跑弯道外圈。"

"嗯，这我懂。"安德鲁答道。

"啊,你懂,你懂。"琼斯说道。"那就好,祝你好运,小伙子。"

安德鲁边走边回过头来。"只要我能跑进二分,"他有点儿不自在地说道,"那就意味着——很多。"

安德鲁离开了他,独自一人走进广场花园吃三明治。这是个晴朗的初夏,可是他却因为紧张和孤独感到凉飕飕的。他坐了四十分钟的公共汽车去运动场,他想早点儿到那里,半英里比赛时间定在三点。

他有多少胜算?他已经在前一天晚上的分组赛中以二分六秒的成绩出线,可这却没有任何意义。乔·布鲁斯特在他的后面,但他是在保存实力。佩里和雷德布鲁克在另一场分组赛中打了个平手,成绩都是二分五秒。谁都不可小觑。最可怕的是他发现自己开始用力过猛,遥遥领先,结果腿疲劳得最后无法完成比赛。他以前从来没有跟雷德布鲁克这样的高级赛跑选手对过阵。

上了公共汽车以后,他尽量克制自己不去想比赛。太紧张一点儿用处也没有。可这是个千载难逢的机会啊。

哎呀,他要是跑好了,今天取得了名次,他的名字就会上当地的报纸《哨兵》。老人们也愿意看到这样的结果。假如他可以跑进二分钟,嗯,将来总有一天,在他有生之年,他会做到的。那将是了不起的成就。它会给他信心,会让他更有影响力。

伴随着这样愉快的幻想,公共汽车慢吞吞地走着。安德鲁一手提着包,在一点半的时候抵达了运动场。看到诸如六便士看台座位入口和一先令看台座位入口这样的设施,都让他感觉怪怪的。这让他感觉自己是至关重要的,因为就像观众为了看自己比赛而买票一样。实际上,他是第一个进更衣室换衣服的赛手。他慢吞吞地换着,把衣服放到角落里的一张长凳上。他小心翼翼地穿上了钉子鞋,走到外面的跑道上。他以前习惯在普通运动场跑，普通运动场跑四圈是一英里，而这个运动场是三圈一英里。可惜啊：赛跑中的每个陌生之处都是一个小的干扰因素。不仅如此，这个运动场还没有四个角，却有两条直道，两端是长长的半圆形跑道。

安德鲁找到了半英里起跑线，判明了一下方位。他慢跑了半圈，冲刺了一两次，然后做了做呼吸训练。他在终点直道上踱来踱去。他在这里必须冲到前面。他决意找个真正的冲刺起点，要不惜任何代价跑到安全距离之内。用不着老琼斯告诉他不要跑弯道的外圈。此时已经是两点多了，有一两个人进了看台。第一场比赛两点半开始。他回到更衣室，发现里面到处都是人，吵吵嚷嚷，你推我搡的。他感觉很不自在，就又出来了。但愿他能熬过去，还要等四十五分钟。桌子上赤身躺着一个人，按摩师在按摩。安德鲁排队等着按摩。这似乎挺专业的。

"该你啦。"按摩师招呼他。

安德鲁脱下了背心。

"把裤子也脱了。"

他有点儿不好意思地把松松垮垮的休闲裤脱了下来，趴在了桌子上。

"先按摩正面，老兄。"按摩师说道。

这似乎有些不雅，不过安德鲁还是翻过身来。

按摩师把他的肚子敲得砰砰响，接着敲他的背，然后敲他的臀部，还有他的大腿、小腿，涂抹一种味道很冲的油，增强皮肤的活力，刺激神经。不错。

他看到布鲁斯特和佩里在说话，就过去攀谈，说了句与半英里比赛有关的话，可是他们似乎已经记不起来他是谁了。他找了个座位独自坐着。但愿能早点儿熬过去。

一个红脸汉猛地把门打开。

"百码比赛的都出来。"他大声喊道。

"知道他是谁吗？"有人说道，"他是梅杰·卡利夫——参加过国际田径赛的老选手。"

百码比赛的选手急匆匆地出去了。一百个人分四五组。安德鲁透过更衣室的窗户向外望去，却还是分心走神，看不出赛况。他特别难受。

最后，百码比赛结束了。一分钟，或者大约一分钟慢吞吞地过去了。安德鲁站起来又坐下，第五次把鞋带系紧。接下来，门猛地被推开了，梅杰·卡利夫第二次朝屋里看了看，大声喊道："半英里的都出来！"

与此同时，他听到外面铃声大作，听起来命运攸关。这意味着下一场比赛的开始。运动场上的所有观众都在翻看节目单，在读节目单上运动员的名字。随着叮叮当当的铃声渐渐消失，安德鲁感到恐怖也渐渐逼近了。他一跃而起，穿过更衣室直奔门口。

此时，又遇到一个新的尴尬情况：为什么其他赛跑手没起身？他等了一会儿，想跟他们一起走，可是他们似乎都有鞋或者绑带要在这最后一分钟整理。

"嗳，我想我们最好上场吧。"

"稍等，乔，"佩里说道，"我一定要戴上护膝。"

安德鲁痛苦地在更衣室的门口徘徊。他们为什么不赶紧出来跑完算了？他恨不得马上跑完比赛，省得受煎熬了。最后，他发觉再这么拉着门很傻，于是他出了门走到外面的混凝土过道上。他自然不能独自一人上跑道，也不能再回更衣室，于是他靠着墙，尽量把思想放空。

别人都在干什么？"哦，不要胡思乱想，"他低声自言自语，"哦，不要胡思乱想！"下次比赛他就会找个更合适的时间起来，不会在一起比赛的赛跑手起来之前就起来了。

走廊尽头的阳光隐去了，梅杰从他身边擦过。

"那些跑半英里的人在哪里？"他态度和蔼地问安德鲁。

"我想——"安德鲁开了口，却发现梅杰却根本没想听他回答。

梅杰打开了门，安德鲁瞥到他们在站着说东道西，好像根本没把比赛当回事儿。

"跑半英里的都上场——请大家快点儿。"梅杰说道。

他们这次出来了，安德鲁心跳如捣，加入了他们的队伍。

"啊，布鲁斯特，"梅杰问道，"你今天要给我们秀什么啊？"

"没指望你注意到我，"布鲁斯特答道，"发令枪一响，第一个六百码我就争取咬住小雷德布鲁克，我就是想看看我的能力！"

这听起来很随意，可安德鲁强烈地感觉到了布鲁斯特的言外之意："我认为自己是半英里的高级赛跑手。我坚信自己可以跑过雷德布鲁克。我对剩下的人都不屑一顾。"

安德鲁小心得不能再小心地踏上了跑道。在户外，他感觉好多了。然后，他扫了眼身后巨大的看台，心中大为震惊，只见看台上座无虚席，密密麻麻的，观众都在看他，等着看他跑。

随着铃声响起，看台上的观众让安德鲁的心中涌起了一种新的可怕意味。对于运动会上的人山人海，他早已司空见惯。他曾经跟这些观众坐在一起，观看运动场中央的赛跑手和屈指可数的官员。运动场中央是人山人海这幅画不可分割的组成部分。

他从来没想到过踏进竞技场那一刻就闯入画面。此时，这幅画里只有人山人海，别无他物。不论他朝四面八方哪个方向看，只能看到一张张人脸、一双双盯着他的眼睛和一堆堆的帽子。

他眼睛盯着地面，离开跑道穿过草地向起跑线走去。半英里比赛，赛程一圈半，所以起跑线距离大看台最远。半圈之后所到达的看台，正是比赛进入精彩阶段的地方，到时候，人人都会开始有紧张感，那些认真的人开始你追我赶,奋勇争先。跑完剩下的整整一圈以后,又会回到大看台所在的地方。

安德鲁沿着脚下的路走向运动场的中部,这里离人山人海就没有那么近了。夏天依然新鲜,依然可以给感官带来惊喜。他轻轻地踏上弹性跑道。青草闻起来有清新的味道。此后多年,只要一闻到青草的清新味道,都会让他想起这一刻,让他心生忐忑。

清新的空气拍打着他的头和喉咙,在他裸露的双腿上嬉戏。

安德鲁看到其他半英里赛跑手在跑道附近慢跑,时不时会有人舒展着肌肉向前冲刺。安德鲁想高抬腿慢跑来放松双腿,可是感觉太不自在,腿抬不起来。

他率先来到起跑点,紧接着是另一场痛苦的等待。其他人还在跑道附近蹦蹦跳跳。比赛什么时候才能开始啊?神经紧张肯定会对四肢的力量有损害吧?最后,发令员终于来了。

"今天是个试跑的好天气,"他对安德鲁说道,"让我觉得退出很傻,我羡慕你们这些小子。"

安德鲁太痛苦了,说不出话来,于是他点了点头算是回答。

"你要是想得个名次,"一个发令员说道,"就听我给你支招,看住雷德布鲁克,他可能会在一开始就超过布鲁斯特,让布鲁斯特大吃一惊。你看,那是因为他知道自己没有能力冲刺。"

安德鲁又点了点头。当然,这是一个预料之中的结局,比赛里只有雷德布鲁克和布鲁斯特,谁也不会想到他。

其他人开始陆陆续续地到了。安德鲁脱掉了羊毛衫。这次他又来早了。其他人还在等。大家现在都不说话了。

雷德布鲁克跟一个官员漫步穿过运动场。他抬头看了看,然后突然轻快地慢跑起来。

安德鲁脸上还有清风拂面。人海里的低语声穿过运动场，传到他的耳畔。一个报童在大声叫卖。

赛跑手们中依然没有一个人说话。他们一个接一个地默默脱掉了运动夹克和羊毛衫。大家熟知的布鲁斯特俱乐部的标志服色出现了——胸部有带状的红黑色。雷德布鲁克脚步轻快地跑了过来，大家都没察觉。

"对不起，"他说道，他穿着阿基里斯俱乐部服色的运动夹克突然冒了出来。安德鲁扫了一眼自己朴素的白色运动服，比雷德布鲁克的长，比雷德布鲁克的紧。

赛跑手们互相审视着，在跑道上各就各位。雷德布鲁克比安德鲁稍微高一点，身材完美。他蓬松的玉米色头发剪得短短的，比他棕褐色的脸色淡一号。他的四肢闪耀着青春和力量的光芒。他的一举一动迅疾如火。

难怪他这么能跑，安德鲁暗想，他必胜无疑。

"我会说各就各位——预备——然后发令枪。"

终于开始了，安德鲁想。此刻他的心都快要从嗓子眼里跳出来了。

一秒钟艰难地挨过去了。

安德鲁跪下来准备起跑冲刺。

"预备！"

他的膝盖在打战，离开了跑道，现在是靠脚趾和关节在保持平衡，他由于紧张在颤抖。

砰。

你追我赶。摩肩接踵。一定要脱离其他赛跑手。

安德鲁摆脱了别人，疾驰向前，全速前进。他转向里道。迄今为止，一切顺利。他已经占据了里道，而且还领先。他会赢得这场比赛吗？他已经适应了大步跑，速度快却很轻松。

他平静地用鼻子呼吸。尽管比赛已经开始了，他还是感到紧张万分，不过，此刻是一种令人兴奋的紧张了。他看着与跑道相接的草皮的青草的每个叶片。一个体育场管理员把一个白色涂料桶放了下来。

　　安德鲁意识到自己已经以快速的步伐打败对手，于是他转换成慢速大步。迄今为止，一切都在按计划按部就班地进行，他也开始有了信心。

　　就在他们第一次接近观众席和第二个长长的直道弯道的时候，他发现佩里慢慢地在他的外道出现了。安德鲁吃了一惊，不由得心生忧虑。在他以往所跑过的半英里比赛里，只要按照既定的步伐跑，就保证可以领先。他决定保持步伐不变，而佩里一大步接着一大步地从他身边过去了，开始领先。安德鲁继续按照自己的步伐跑，与佩里拉开了一两码的距离。

　　就在他们往弯道上跑的时候，突然响起了噼啪噼啪的脚步声，安德鲁发现布鲁斯特填补了他与佩里之间的空白。其他人都纷纷靠近，他意识到整个运动场上的运动员都比他跑得快。他稍稍加快了速度，试探地从外圈想再次超过布鲁斯特。就在他就要超过布鲁斯特的时候，弯道到了。他还不至于笨到在弯道的时候跑外圈，于是他再次放慢步伐返回里道。可是就在他想到这里的一瞬间，后面的赛跑手不费吹灰之力地靠近并且迅速赶上了布鲁斯特，安德鲁这才意识到雷德布鲁克已经抢占了里道。安德鲁只得在转弯的时候跑外圈了。"大傻瓜！"他对自己说道。

　　那一刻，人山人海里的琼斯和一两个经验丰富的赛跑手心领神会地交换了一下目光，其余观众对于安德鲁表现出的这个小技术性失误没有概念。

　　就这样，他们绕起了那个长长的弯道。佩里领先，步伐依然紧迫；布鲁斯特第二，对于应该跑什么样的步伐没有特别清晰的概念，只是下定决心不输给佩里;雷德布鲁克明智地保持在攻击距离以内,而安德鲁和另外两个赛跑手则不舒服地在雷德布鲁克的外圈挤着。

他们跑出长长的弯道,完成了一半赛程的时候,安德鲁彻底乱了阵脚。他以前跑半英里赛从来没有这么紧张过。氧气不够,连呼吸都困难了。他此刻不是在用鼻子平稳地呼吸了。已经有一种让人吃惊的衰弱感觉在大腿的正面出现了。现在想占优势已经没有希望了。让他欣慰的是,他又转回了里道,跟在雷德布鲁克的后面了。他们已经跑了大约一分钟——却好像过了一个世纪。他还能不能保持这个速度再坚持一段时间?在他面前,长长的直道延展开来,直道的尽头是运动场那片长长的弯道,弯道过后才到终点直道。然后是冲刺,而他已经感到连一点点冲刺的力量都没有了。

他看着雷德布鲁克的双脚,跟着跑,一步又一步。

而此刻,要跟住雷德布鲁克,他还必须加快速度了。每跑一步,雷德布鲁克的背影就离他远一些。他挣扎着把步伐迈大,却无济于事。雷德布鲁克已经遥遥领先。此时他跟布鲁斯特齐头并进了。此时他跟佩里齐头并进了。此时他领先。

从大观众席上看,雷德布鲁克在非终点直道上跑得是多么轻松自如啊!"跑得真好看!"人们交头接耳。"正是该加速的地方。""判断准确!""看他怎么渐入佳境,跑最后的弯道吧。"

而这也是安德鲁要提速的地方。他此时已经把自己以前的种种计划忘了个一干二净。加速已经是不可能的了。后面的人中有一个轻松地从他身旁跑过,填补了雷德布鲁克与他之间留下的空白。第六个人跑到了他的外圈。背后有一种空荡荡的感觉,他此时跑在最后面。

此刻,他们跑到了终点直道前的最后弯道上了。他的腿好像一点儿力气也没有了。他喘不上来气,嘴里咕哝着。大腿的无力感变成了抽筋似的痛感。与此同时，他一直眼睁睁地看着与雷德布鲁克距离越来越远，一会儿是整整五码，紧接着是八码，不由得隐隐约约地感到绝望。佩里落回第三名了，布鲁斯特在追赶雷德布鲁克。

模模糊糊的隐痛阵阵袭来，安德鲁感到无助，无助。

他还要跑得有节制。他要强迫自己的双腿迈轻松自然的大步。当他唯一的希望就是最后疯狂的冲刺的时候，他的身体却还必须被迫有节制地跑下去，这是赛跑最难熬的时候，是噩梦时刻。

"加油，"他鼓励自己，"再跑五十五码——勇气，老兄——勇气。"

若是安德鲁知道别人此时此刻的感觉的话，他就会信心百倍了。在比赛的第一个四分之一赛程里，多亏安德鲁自己兴奋起来了，他比别人跑得快，而别人也没有在意。雷德布鲁克由于缺乏节制，感觉在四分之一英里的标志处就已经上气不接下气了。他也怀疑自己是否有力量做最后的冲刺。于是，他决定趁着自己还有冲刺的力气，提前来个出人意料的加速。他们一到弯道，在距离赛跑终点三百码的地方，他就使出最大的力气加速，高速前进。在佩里和布鲁斯特还没弄清楚怎么回事之前，他已经拉开了五码、八码的距离，遥遥领先了。对于这一切，观众比参加比赛的人看得更清楚。

他们此时都上了直道，安德鲁以为雷德布鲁克在重整旗鼓做最后的冲刺。而事实恰恰相反，他在苦苦地死撑，苟延残喘。他那欢快的步伐已经转瞬不再，他的大步已经迈得毫无生气，大腿的冲刺肌肉已经一点力量都没有了。他在挣扎，每迈一大步都要自己问自己："我行吗？我行吗？我行吗？毫无疑问，每一步都离终点越来越近了。我能坚持到最后吗？"

佩里已经跑得筋疲力尽，无以复加了。在最后三十码，布鲁斯特一直拼命追赶雷德布鲁克，却根本找不到节奏。

在拐那个能把人累死的弯道时，整个运动场上唯一懂得合理使用剩余体力的人是安德鲁。只剩四十码了，他现在可以竭尽全力，最后拼命地放手一搏了。再次加速。此刻距离直道是三十码——二十码，突然，他的自控土崩瓦解了。他在用体内的全部力量疯狂地拼搏。

在距离直道十码的时候，他看到自己在比赛中的命运彻底反转了。他已经成功冲刺了一次！他外道上的那个人看不见了。上了直道以后，他从外道击败了前面的那个人。又跑过了几码，他击败了摇摇晃晃的佩里。

他已经跑到了第三名。他四肢力量倍增。"加油，加油！加速，你能追上布鲁斯特。齐头并进。感觉到了他的挣扎。他跑不过你。把他拿下！"

在遥远、遥远的某个地方，有一种狂乱的剧痛：别人的剧痛。几英里以外的跑道旁有一张脸。

此刻该拿下第二个人了，第二个人，他能追上雷德布鲁克。可他能及时追上他吗？他们此刻已经跑过了一百码的起跑线：只剩一百码了。他能吗？他能吗？他的第一个辉煌的冲刺已经完成了。身体痛苦而虚弱，他要再一次跟拖后腿的身体做斗争。而他正在一步一步地做。他紧握着拳头，强迫冲刺得筋疲力尽的肌肉奋起。

奇怪的是，时间分秒不差地在延长，直道在延长。又跑了五码，此刻四码，此刻三码。

雷德布鲁克听到了他的声音，接着感觉到他在逼近：在后面二码处，此刻在肩并肩。他再一次拼尽全力发力。他们一起快速跑过一百码的终点线，距离半英里终点线的棉线还有十码，耳畔是看台观众低沉的吼叫声。雷德布鲁克看到自己被击败了，却也跟到了最后一步。

接下来，安德鲁领先了。

长长的白色的羊毛终点线被自己的胸撞开,面对辉煌的战绩,他满心欢喜。

"你成功啦,你成功啦!"令人难以置信的珍贵瞬间。

接着,他昏昏沉沉地倒在了跑道上。

几个强壮的胳膊把他拉了起来,搀扶着他走向草地。"干得好,冲刺非常漂亮!"他听到有人说。他又倒了下来,这次是坐了下来。周围天旋地转。雷德布鲁克站着呢,还没有累坏。

疼,这双腿,还有大腿肌肉多疼啊!必须站起来,见鬼!就算你赢了又怎样?

雷德布鲁克向安德鲁走了过来,脸上带着笑容,表情克制。

"干得好,"他说道,"把我赢得很漂亮。"

"啊唷,"安德鲁叫道,还气喘吁吁的,"大腿肌肉,"他起身,一瘸一拐地走来走去。他感觉腿怪怪的。臀部的肌肉疼得可怕。

雷德布鲁克笑了:"我知道这种感觉,"他说道,"由于缺乏训练造成的!"

"哦,我有过一点点训练,"安德鲁说道,"实际上有一定的量呢。你知道跑了多长时间吗?"

"一分五十九秒四," 雷德布鲁克告诉他。"我刚刚进二分。我必须说我们为第一季赛事取得了不错的成绩。"

"一分五十九秒四,"安德鲁说道,"真的吗?"

一个裁判向他们走了过来。

其他人走了过来。他们说的都一样。

"你不早冲刺,到底是什么原因?"

"我不知道有没有冲刺的能力。"安德鲁解释道。

布鲁斯特加入了这群人。

"嗯,这是我最后一次参加半英里比赛,"他说道。"我这辈子以前从来都没有被迫跑得这么快过。"

可是,显而易见,他很高兴。他在雷德布鲁克后面到达终点,距离雷德布鲁克大约十码,所以成绩大约是二分二秒或者二分三秒。

此时,安德鲁完完全全地开心起来。身心特别愉快特别放松,特别心满意足地观看其他比赛。他交了不少新朋友。然后,他走进更衣室,泡在蒸汽浴里,抽着烟,跟隔间的布鲁斯特大声说着话。生活特别和美。

他从浴室走了出来,来到运动场上,跟他看到的每个人聊天:一次又一次地讨论他参加的这场比赛;喝了三四杯啤酒;铺张浪费,乱花了几先令。他惊讶地看到,雷德布鲁克又在四分之一英里比赛中出现了,以五十一秒二的成绩,以微弱优势夺取了另一个累人的比赛的第一名。安德鲁第一个过去拍了拍他的后背。

"了不起的成绩,"他说道。"我纳闷儿你跑完半英里以后怎么还能取得这么好的成绩!"

"哦,这个," 雷德布鲁克答道,"这场比赛让我放松了。你为什么不参加,懒鬼?"

在坐公共汽车回家的路上,安德鲁靠在椅背上一口又一口使劲儿抽着烟斗。他第一次独自把比赛的过程在脑子里过了一遍。嗯,他跑赢了。此刻,他觉得世界上任何事都不在话下。

说到底,赛跑是人们常做的事情。足球,以及其他比赛来了又去了。一个优秀的赛跑手是超越时代的,几百年,几千年以后,还会有他这样的赛跑手。而他,安德鲁,是一个优秀的赛跑手,一个高级赛跑手。一分五十九秒四,太棒啦!

因为疲劳和兴奋,又喝了点儿啤酒,他的头有点儿晕眩。他靠在椅背上,就像在这个星球上最幸福的人那样——轻叹了一声。

The Half Mile

By T. O. Beachcroft

Saturday noon. The town-hall clock boomed the hour in the distance. All over the town hooters called to each other from street to street. From the gates of twenty different potteries men, women, boys, and girls streamed. Ones and twos grew to a steady flow, then died away again to ones and twos.

Andrew Williamson, a dipper at the Royal Chorley, was stopped at the gate by old Jones the doorkeeper.

"So long, Andrew," he said, "good luck for the half mile."

Andrew glanced at him, and looked away self-consciously.

"How did you know I was running?"

"Oh, I takes an interest," said Jones, "used to run a half mile myself."

"Go on?" said Andrew, "I never knew."

"I was good for one fifty-eight," said the old man. "That was good going in those days."

"Go on?" said Andrew again, "but that's class running. That's a class half mile."

"Oh, I dunno, plenty on 'em do it now!"

"Well, I wish I could. That's my ambition: to get inside two minutes, I've never beaten two four yet!"

"Well, this is just the day for it," the veteran told him. "You have a nice trot round first: get some good summer air into your lungs: you'll win."

"But I've never run in a class race," Andrew persisted. "I've only done Club races. I can't hope for more'n a place; look who's running."

"Who?" said Jones.

"Well, there's six of us in the final. Let's see: Joe Brewster, the cross-country man, he can run a four thirty mile, and now he wants to try the half."

"Well, he'll never do minutes," said Jones, "take it from me."

"Then there's Perry, him as ran at the 'Three Clubs' meet at Derby last week. He did two four then."

"Well, who else?"

"There's that Redbrooke, the Cambridge Blue. I ain't got an earthly."

"He's a fine runner," said Jones, "but d'you think he's trained in May? Not likely. It'll be his first time out, trial spin like. Are you trained?"

"Pretty good," said Andrew, "been at it evenings all the month. Had a good race a week ago."

"Take it from me," Jones told him slowly, "stick to Redbrooke. He'll come up at the end of the first quarter. You watch 'im. Don't mind what the others do. And don't run on the outside round bends."

"Well, I know enough for that," said Andrew.

"Ah, you know, you know." said Jones. "Well, good luck, lad."

Andrew turned back again as he was going. "If I could ever beat two minutes," he said a little self-consciously, "it'd mean—oh, well, a hellov a lot."

Andrew left him and went alone into the square garden to eat his sandwiches. It was a bright early summer day, yet now that, he was alone he felt chilly with nerves. He had a forty minutes' bus ride to the ground, and he meant to get there early. The half mile was timed for three.

What chance had he got? He had won his heat in two six the evening before, but that meant nothing. Joe Brewster was behind him, but he'd only paced out, he knew. Perry and Redbrooke had tied the other heat in two five. There was nothing to go by. Dreadful if he found himself outclassed and run off his legs. He had never been up against a class man before—a fellow like Redbrooke.

Once in the bus he tried his best not to think of the race. No good getting too much of a needle. Yet it was a big chance.

Why, if he did well, if he was placed in the race today, his name would be in the Sentinel. The old uns would like to see that, too. If he could beat two minutes—well, he would someday, before he died. That would be doing something really big. It would give him confidence. It would make him stronger altogether.

The bus jogged along with such pleasant fancies. Andrew reached the ground, bag in hand, at half past one. It gave him a queer feeling to see "Sixpence Entrance" on the gates, and "This stand a shilling", and the like. It made him feel very responsible that people should pay to come to the sport that he was providing. He was practically the first comer in the changing room. He changed slowly, putting his clothes on a bench in the corner. He put on his spiked shoes with elaborate care and went out on the track. It was three laps to the mile instead of the four he was used to. Pity: every strangeness was a little disturbing in a race. There were not four corners either, but two long straights with a long semicircular sweep at each end.

Andrew found the half mile start, and took his bearing. He trotted round half a lap, took one or two sprints, then some breathing exercises. He paced up the back straight. That was where he must come up to the front. He determined to make a real sprinting start, and get an inside berth at all costs. No need for old Jones to tell him not to run on the outside round bends. It was past two by now. One or two people were coming into the stands, the first event being at 2.30. When he got back to the changing room he found it full of a noisy jostling crowd. He felt rather strange, and out of it. If only he could get it over. Three quarters of an hour to wait still. On a table a naked body was being massaged. Andrew waited his turn for a rub. This seemed really professional.

"Your turn, sir," said the rubber.

Andrew stripped off his vest.

"Might as well take your bags off, too."

He divested himself a bit shyly, and lay face downwards on the table.

"Front side first, old man," said the rubber.

It seemed a bit indecent, but Andrew turned over.

The man pommeled his stomach, then his back, then his buttocks, his thighs, and his calves, rubbing in a strong-smelling oil that gingered up his skin and made his nerves tingle. Good.

He saw Brewster and Perry talking and made a remark to them about the half mile, but they did not seem to remember who he was. He found himself a seat alone. If only he could get it over.

A red-faced man thrust the door open.

"All out for the hundred," he shouted.

"Know who that is?" someone said. "That's Major Cunliffe—the old international."

The hundred-yards men trooped out. There were four or five heats in the hundred. Andrew watched out of the changing room window, but he couldn't concentrate and took no stock of what happened. He was acutely miserable.

At last the hundred yards was finished. A minute or so dragged by. Andrew stood up and sat down again and fastened his shoes for the fifth time. Then the door burst open and Major Cunliffe looked in again: "All out for the half mile!"

At the same time he heard a bell ringing outside. It sounded fateful. It meant next event due. All over the ground people were turning over their programs and reading the names. As the clangor died away Andrew felt something approaching terror. He sprang to his feet and crossed towards the door.

Now a new awkwardness arose. Why did none of the other half milers move? He waited for a moment for them to join him, but each man of them seemed to have found some last-minute adjustment to a shoe or bandage.

"Well," said Brewster, "I suppose we'd better be moving."

"Wait a bit, Joe," said Perry, "I must get my ankle strap on."

Andrew hovered miserably in the doorway of the changing room. Why couldn't they buck up and get it over? If only he could get it over. At last, finding it ridiculous to hold the door open any longer, he went through it and waited outside in the concrete passage. He certainly could not walk on to the track without the others, nor could he go back into the changing room. He leant against the wall trying to think of nothing.

What could the others be doing? "Oh, come on," he murmured, "come on!" Next time he would know better than to get up before the other men in his race were on the move.

The sunlight end of the passage was suddenly eclipsed and the Major brushed by him.

"Where are those half milers?" he said genially to Andrew.

"I thinks——" began Andrew, but found an answer was not expected.

The Major opened the door, and Andrew caught a glimpse of the bunch of them standing and talking as if the race meant nothing.

"Everyone out for the half mile——come on, please," said the Major.

This time they came and with beating heart Andrew joined them.

"Well, Brewster," said the Major, "what are you going to show us today?"

"Don't expect you'll notice me," said Brewster, "after the gun's gone. I shall try and stick to young Redbrooke for the first six hundred, anyhow. I only want to see what I can do!"

It sounded splendidly casual, but Andrew had a strong feeling that what Brewster meant was: "I rather fancy myself as a class half miler, so just watch me. I believe I can beat Redbrooke. I'm not troubling about the rest, anyhow."

Andrew stepped gingerly along the track. He felt rather better at being in the open air. Then he glanced behind him at the grand stand. He received a shock. It was full—full of banks of people looking at him, waiting to see him run.

As with the bell, the audience rushed on Andrew with a terrific new meaning. He had often seen large crowds at sports meetings. He had sat with them and watched the runners and the few officials in the center of the ground. The center of the ground had always appeared to be part of the whole picture with the crowd.

It had never occurred to him for a moment that to step in the arena was to break that unit. Now the whole picture was crowd and nothing else. Wherever he raised his eyes on all sides of him, he saw nothing but a bank of staring faces, a mob of hats and faces.

With eyes fixed on the ground, he left the track and began to walk across the grass towards the start. The half mile, being a lap and a half, led off at the farthest point from the grand stand. The half lap brought it round to the stand just at the stage where the race was getting into its stride, when everybody was beginning to feel the collar and those who meant business were jostling for places in front. The remaining complete lap brought the finish round to the grand stand again.

Andrew's path took him into the middle of the ground; here the crowd was less imminent. The summer was still new enough to greet the senses with surprise. He stepped lightly on the elastic turf. The grass breathed out delicious freshness. For years afterwards that fragrance was to set Andrew's nerves tingling with the apprehension of this moment.

The lively air fanned his head and throat. It played about his bare legs.

Andrew saw the other half milers were trotting round the track. Occasionally one would shoot forward in a muscle-stretching burst. Andrew tried a high-stepping trot across the grass to flex his own legs, but was too self-conscious to keep it up.

He reached the starting point first. Another agonizing wait followed. The others were still capering round the ash path. Would he never get it over? Surely the tension of nerves must rack the strength from his limbs? At last the starter approached.

"Jolly day for a trial spin," he told Andrew. "Makes me feel an old fool to be out of it. I envy you boys."

Andrew felt too miserable to answer. He nodded.

"If you want a place," said a starter, "take my advice and watch Redbrooke. He'll probably try and take Brewster off his legs early—he knows he can't sprint, you see."

Andrew nodded again. Of course it was a foregone conclusion that only Redbrooke and Brewster were in the race. No one had a thought for him.

The others began to arrive. Andrew stripped off his sweater. Again he was premature. The others waited. All were silent now.

Redbrooke was strolling across the ground with one of the officials. He looked up and broke into a brisk trot.

The air still freshened Andrew's face. Across the ground he could hear the murmur of the crowd. A paper boy was shouting.

Still none of the runners spoke. In silence, one by one, they took off blazers and sweaters. The well-known colors of Brewster's club appeared—a red and black band round the chest. Redbrooke cantered up unconcerned.

"Sorry," he said, and emerged from his blazer in Achilles Club colors. Andrew glanced at his plain white things, longer and tighter than Redbrooke's.

The runners eyed each other as they took their places on the track. Redbrooke was a shade taller than Andrew and perfectly formed. His corn-colored hair was a disheveled crop, paler in hue than the tan of his face. His limbs flashed with youth and strength. His poise was quick as flame.

No wonder he can run, thought Andrew. He must win.

"I shall say on your marks—set—and then fire."

At last, thought Andrew. His heart was beating in his throat now.

A second toiled by.

Andrew dropped to his knee for a sprinting start.

"Set!"

His knee quivered up from the track. It was toes and knuckles now, a balance quivering with tautness.

Crash.

Scurry. Shoulders jostling. Mind out.

Andrew shot clear, going at top speed. He swung into the inside place. So far so good. He'd got his inside place, and the lead too. Was he to make the running? Hesettied down to a stride, fast but easy.

He breathed calmly through his nose. Although the race had started he still felt very nervous—an exhilarating nervousness now. He saw each blade of grass where out turf edge met track. A groundsman set down a whitewash pail.

Andrew realized he was cutting out too fast a pace. He swung into a slower stride. So far all had gone according to plan, and he began to take courage.

As they approached the pavilion for the first time and the second long corner of the race, he found Perry was creeping up on his outside. Andrew was surprised and a little worried. In all the half miles he had run before the pace he had set would have assured him the lead. He decided to make no effort, and Perry passed stride by stride and dropped into the lead. Andrew continued at his own pace, and a gap of a yard or two opened.

As they came on to the bend there was a sudden sputter of feet and Andrew found that Brewster had filled the gap. Others were coming up and he realized that the whole field was moving faster than he was. He quickened up slightly and swung out tentatively to pass Brewster again. Before he could pass, the corner was reached. He at least knew better than to run on the outside round the curve; so he slackened again to pull back into the inside. But in the very thought of doing so, the runner behind closed smoothly and swiftly up to Brewster, and Andrew saw that Redbrooke had got his inside berth. Andrew had to take the curve on the outside.

"Blinking fool" he told himself.

Old Jones and one or two other experienced runners in the crowd caught each other's eyes for a moment; the rest of the audience had no notion of the little display of bad technique that Andrew had given.

So they went round the long curve. Perry in the lead and still pressing the pace; Brewster second, with no very clear notion of what the pace ought to be, and determined not to lose Perry; Redbrooke keeping wisely within striking distance, and Andrew bunched uncomfortably on the outside of Redbrooke with two others.

By the time they came out of the long bend and completed the first half of the race Andrew was thoroughly rattled. Never had he felt such a strain at this stage of a half mile. Already it was difficult to get enough air; he was no longer breathing evenly through his nose. Already a numbing weakness was creeping down the front of his thighs. Hopeless now to think of gaining ground. With relief he found he was able to drop into the inside again behind Redbrooke. They had now been running for about one minute—it seemed an age. Could he possibly stick to it for another period, as long again? The long stretch of straight in front of him, the long sweep of curve at the end of the ground that only brought you at the beginning of the finishing straight. Then the sprint. Already he felt he could not find an ounce of sprint.

Pace by pace he stuck to it watching Redbrooke's feet.

But even now he must quicken up if he was to hold Redbrooke. At each step Redbrooke's back was leaving him. He struggled to lengthen but it was useless. Redbrooke was moving up to the front. Now he was equal with Brewster; now with Perry; now he was in the lead.

How easy Redbrooke's move down the back straight looked from the grand stand. "Pretty running," people told each other. "Just the place to come up." "Nicely judged." "See how he worked himself through from the last corner."

And this was the very place at which Andrew had meant to move up himself. He remembered nothing of his plans now. It was impossible to increase his effort. One of the men behind came smoothly by and dropped into the gap that Redbrooke had left in front of him. The sixth man came up on his outside. There was a kind of emptiness at his back. He was running equal last.

Now they came into the final curve before the finishing straight. His legs seemed powerless. He grunted for breath. The weakness in his thighs had grown to a cramping pain. And all the time with dull despair he saw Redbrooke going up, now five yards clear, now eight. Perry had dropped back to third, and Brewster was chasing Redbrooke.

Dark waves of pain swept over Andrew. Hopeless. Hopeless.

Still he must keep running with control. He must force his legs to a smooth long stride. This was the worst part of any race; nightmare moments, when the only hope was a last frenzied dash, yet still the body must be forced along with conscious control.

"Come on," he told himself, "another fifty yards—guts, man—guts."

Had only Andrew known what the others were feeling, he would have taken courage. The whole pace of the first quarter, thanks to Andrew's own excitement, had been faster than anyone cared for. Redbrooke, untrained as he was, had found himself badly winded at the quarter-mile mark. He, too, doubted whether he could have any punch left at the finish. He determined, therefore, to make a surprise effort early, when he still had a powerful sprint in him. As soon as they came into the curve, he stepped on the gas as hard as he could, three hundred yards from home, and steamed away. He jumped a lead of five, eight, ten yards before Perry or Brewster realized what was happening. It was a thing the crowd could follow better than the men in the race.

Now as they came into the straight, Andrew thought Redbrooke was gathering himself for a final dash. Far from it; he was hanging on for grim death. His sparkling effort had died right away. His stride was nerveless. The sprinting muscles in his thighs had lost every ounce of their power. He was struggling and asking himself at every stride: "Can I, can I, can I—surely those steps are drawing nearer—can I last it?"

Perry was desperately run out. Brewster had already been chasing Redbrooke hard for the last thirty yards, but could not find any pace at all.

Andrew alone of the field had he known it had been nursing his remnant of strength round that grueling bend. Only forty yards to go now and he could throw all he had into a last desperate effort. Keep it Up just a moment more. Thirty yards to the straight now—twenty—suddenly his control was shattered. He was fighting in a mindless fury of effort for every ounce of strength in him.

In ten yards he saw his whole fortune in the race change. He had got a sprint then! The man on his outside vanished. He raced round the outside of the fellow in front hand over fist as he came into the straight. In another few yards he had the faltering Perry taped.

He had already run into third place. New strength surged through his limbs. "Come on, come on: up, you can catch Brewster. Level. Feel him struggling. He can't hold you. Got him!"

Far, far off, a distant frenzied pain, somewhere: someone else's pain. Miles away a face on the side of the track.

Second now. Second, and he could catch Redbrooke. But could he catch him in time? They were past the start of the hundred yards now: a bare hundred to go. Could he? Could he? The first brilliance of his sprint had gone. He was fighting again an agonizing weakness that dragged his legs back. But he was doing it, foot by foot. Fists clenched, to force speed-spent muscles.

Split seconds dragged strange length out. The straight went on and on. Five yards behind, now four, now three.

Redbrooke heard him, then felt him: two yards behind, now at his shoulder. He racked himself for a new effort. Together they swept past the hundred-yards finish, ten yards from the half-mile tape, with the dull roar of the crowd in their ears. Redbrooke saw he was beaten but stuck to it till the last foot.

Then Andrew led.

A splendour of gladness as he watched the stretch of white wool break on his own chest.

"You've done it, you've done it!" Incredible precious moment.

Then he dropped half conscious on the track.

Strong arms plucked him up, and walked him to the grass.

"Well done, very fine finish," he heard. Down again, sitting now. The world swam round you. There was Redbrooke, standing up, not so done then.

Ache, how those legs ache and your thigh muscles, too—must stand up, hell, what does it matter though when you won!

Redbrooke came over to Andrew smiling and controlled.

"Well done," he said, "you had me nicely."

"Ow," said Andrew, still panting, "muscles in my thighs." He got up and limped about. His legs felt absurd. The muscles in his haunches hurt abominably.

Redbrooke smiled. "I know that feeling," he said, "comes of running untrained!"

"Oh, I had trained a bit," said Andrew, "a fair amount really. Do you know what the time was?"

"One fifty-nine and two fifths," Redbrooke told him. "I was just inside two minutes. I must say I think we did fairly well for the first effort of the season."

"One fifty-nine and two fifths," said Andrew, "was it really?"

One of the judges joined them.

Others came up. They all said the same.

"Why on earth didn't you sprint before?"

"No idea I could," explained Andrew.

Brewster joined the group.

"Well, that's my last half mile," he said. "Never had to move so fast in my life before."

But he was obviously pleased. He had finished about ten yards behind Redbrooke and must have done about two two or two three.

Now Andrew began to enjoy himself thoroughly. Gloriously relaxed in mind and body, gloriously contented, he watched the other events. He made new friends. Then he went in and soaked himself in a steaming bath and smoked, shouting to Brewster in the next compartment. Life was very kind.

He came out on to the ground, chatted with everyone he saw: discussed his race a dozen times: had three or four beers: spent a few shillings with wild extravagance. He saw, to his amazement, Redbrooke turn out again for the quarter and fight another grueling finish to win by inches in fifty-one and a fifth seconds. Andrew was the first to pat him on the back.

"Great work," he said. "How you managed it after that half beats me!"

"Oh, well," said Redbrooke, "it loosened me up. Why didn't you come, lazy devil?"

In the bus going home, Andrew leant back and puffed deeply at his pipe. Alone for the first time, he went over the race in his mind. Well, he had done it. He could tackle anything on earth now.

After all running was a thing men had always done. Football, other games, came and went. A good runner was a good runner for all time—with hundreds and hundreds of years of kinship behind him. And he, Andrew, was a good runner. A class runner. One fifty-nine. Damn good!

His head was slightly swimming with fatigue and excitement and beer. He leant back and sighed—as happy as it is possible to be on this planet.

星座决定性格

白羊座——探险家

精力充沛。酷爱冒险、自主性强。自信心爆棚、热情洋溢。

妙趣横生。喜欢挑战。**极端**沉不住气。**有时**自私。

沾火就着。生气勃勃、激情四射、机智过人。

外向。兴趣来得快去得急。自我任性。

勇气可嘉但武断。有肉欲和运动方面的倾向。

金牛座——忍者神龟

魅力无限但有些咄咄逼人。貌似无趣,实则有趣。

工作勤勤恳恳。古道热肠。内心强大,持之以恒。

脚踏实地之人,以自己的方式维稳、保平安。

不找捷径。我美丽,我骄傲。

耐心,靠谱。是良师益友。

爱心多多,心地善良。爱得很用力、激情四射。

内心表达情绪化。有爱大发雷霆的倾向。

矢志不渝。常常自我宠溺。慷慨大方。

双子座——话匣子

聪明伶俐,机智诙谐。外向,健谈话痨。生气勃勃、精力旺盛。

适应能力强,却急需表现自我。能争好辩,还直言不讳。

喜欢改变。多才多艺。忙忙碌碌,有时会紧张兮兮,神经紧张。爱八卦。

会显得肤浅或反复无常。秀外慧中。

巨蟹座——保护神
情绪起伏,有情有义。也许会有些羞涩。非常有爱,非常关爱他人。

靓姐/帅哥。最佳生活伴侣。保护欲强。

创造力强、想象力丰富。小心翼翼。敏感之人。

需要他人关爱。容易受伤但富于同情心。

狮子座——大老板
有条不紊。生活需要井井有条——喜欢掌控一切。

界限分明。倾向于一切都亲力亲为。喜欢发号施令。

乐于助人。善于交际,敞亮。性格外向。

慷慨大方、古道热肠。敏感。富于创造,精力旺盛。

自信满满。爱心多多。狮子认为最重要的是去做正确的事。

魅力无限。

处女座——完美主义者
两性关系中占主导地位。保守守旧。

总是想要刨根问底。能争善辩。常自寻烦恼。聪明绝顶。

讨厌嘈杂和无序。充满希冀。勤奋努力。忠心耿耿。大美人。

会聊天。难取悦。严格苛刻。务实,但非常龟毛。

常常害羞。悲观主义者。

天秤座——和事佬
对遇到的每个人都很好。选择困难。

有独特的吸引力。有创造力、精力充沛,善于交际。

讨厌独处。

安静平和、慷慨大方。爱心多多，貌美。轻佻。

轻言放弃。拖拖拉拉。容易轻信。

双鱼座——梦想家

慷慨大方、心地善良、体贴入微。创造力强，想象力丰富。

也许有时会遮遮掩掩、语义含糊。善解人意。讨厌细节。

爱梦想，不切实际。同情心和爱心爆棚。无私。

接吻技术很好。貌美。

水瓶座——小甜心

乐观主义者，诚实正直。个性讨喜。独立自主。

创造力强，聪颖灵慧。待人友善，忠心耿耿。有时会显得无情。

有时会有一点点叛逆。倔强顽固，但有原创性和独特性。

内在与外在都迷人。性情古怪。

摩羯座——仁人志士

耐心，明智。务实实际，固执刻板。胸怀大志。

有越变越好看的趋势。幽默，搞笑。

有时会有点儿羞答答的，会沉默不语。常态悲观主义者。

摩羯倾向于做事前不过脑，而且有时待人不够友好。

记仇。喜欢与人竞争。志在必得。

天蝎座——小宇宙

精力旺盛。兰心蕙质。有时会有嫉妒心和占有欲。

勤奋努力。接吻大牛。有时会走火入魔或者遮遮掩掩的。

会记仇。有魅力。矢志不渝。

钟爱投身于长久的两性关系。健谈话痨。浪漫。

有时会以自我为中心。激情四射,情绪大起大落。

射手座——逍遥散仙

天生的乐观主义者。不想长大(小飞侠彼得·潘征候群)。

自我宠溺。自负自夸。喜欢奢侈品和赌博。

擅长社交,外向。不喜欢承担责任。常幻想。

没有耐心。爱东游西逛。有许多朋友。轻浮轻佻。

不喜欢守规矩。有时会伪善。

不喜欢受限制——逼仄的空间甚至紧身的衣服。

讨厌被猜疑。秀外慧中。

Constellations Determine Character

ARIES—The Dare devil

Energetic. Adventurous and spontaneous. Confident and enthusiastic.

Fun. Loves a challenge. EXTREMELY impatient. Sometimes selfish.

Short fuse. Lively, passionate, and sharp wit.

Outgoing. Lose interest quickly-easily bored. Egotistical.

Courageous and assertive. Tends to be physical and athletic.

TAURUS—The Enduring One

Charming but aggressive. Can come off as boring, but they are not.

Hard workers. Warm-hearted. Strong, has endurance.

Solid beings who are stable and secure in their ways.

Not looking for shortcuts. Take pride in their beauty.

Patient and reliable. Make great friends and give good advice.

Loving and kind. Loves hard-passionate.

Express themselves emotionally. Prone to ferocious temper-tantrums.

Determined. Indulge themselves often. Very generous.

GEMINI—The Chatterbox

Smart and witty. Outgoing, very chatty. Lively, energetic.

Adaptable but need to express themselves. Argumentative and outspoken.

Like change.Versatile. Busy, sometimes nervous and tense. Gossips.

May seem superficialor inconsistent. Beautiful physically and mentally.

CANCER—The Protector

Moody, emotional. Maybe shy. Very loving and caring.

Pretty/handsome. Excellent partners for life. Protective.

Inventive and imaginative. Cautious. Touchy-feeling kind of person.

Needs love from others. Easily hurt, but sympathetic.

LEO—The Boss

Very organized. Need order in their lives—like being in control.

Like boundaries. Tend to take over everything. Bossy.

Like to help others. Social and outgoing. Extroverted.

Generous, warm-hearted. Sensitive. Creative energy.

Full of themselves. Loving. Doing the right thing is important to Leos.

Attractive.

VIRGO—The Perfectionist

Dominant in relationships. Conservative.

Always wants the last word. Argumentative. Worries. Very smart.

Dislikes noise and chaos. Eager. Hardworking. Loyal. Beautiful. Easy to talk to. Hard to please. Harsh. Practical and very fussy. Often shy. Pessimistic.

LIBRA—The Harmonizer

Nice to everyone they meet. Can't make up their mind.

Have own unique appeal. Creative, energetic, and very social. Hates to be alone.

Peaceful, generous. Very loving and beautiful. Flirtatious.

Give in too easily. Procrastinators. Very gullible.

PISCES—The Dreamer

Generous, kind, and thoughtful. Very creative and imaginative. May become secretive and vague. Sensitive. Don't like details. Dreamy and unrealistic. Sympathetic and loving. Unselfish. Good kisser. Beautiful.

AQUARIUS—The Sweetheart

Optimistic and honest. Sweet personality. Very independent.

Inventive andintelligent. Friendly and loyal. Can seem unemotional.

Can be a bitrebellious. Very stubborn, but original and unique.

Attractive on theinside and out. Eccentric personality.

CAPRICORN—The Go-Getter

Patient and wise. Practical and rigid. Ambitious.

Tends to begood-looking. Humorous and funny.

Can be a bit shy andreserved. Often pessimists.

Capricorns tend to act before they think and can be unfriendly at times.

Hold grudges. Like competition. Get what they want.

SCORPIO—The Intense One

Very energetic. Intelligent. Can be jealous and possessive.

Hardworking. Great kisser. Can become obsessive or secretive.

Holds grudges. Attractive. Determined.

Loves being in long relationships. Talkative. Romantic.

Can be self-centered at times. Passionate and Emotional.

SAGITTARIUS—The Happy-Go-Lucky One

Good-natured optimist. Doesn't want to grow up (Peter Pan Syndrome).

Indulges self. Boastful. Likes luxuries and gambling.

Social and outgoing. Doesn't like responsibilities. Often fantasizes.

Impatient. Fun to bearound. Having lots of friends. Flirtatious.

Doesn't like rules. Sometimes hypocritical.

Dislikes being confined—tight spaces or even tight clothes.

Doesn't like being doubted. Beautiful inside and out.

跟汪星人学做人

若是汪星人当了你的老师

你可能要学习这些功课了

亲人归家,小跑接驾

快乐兜风,一次不拉

体验清风拂面,空气好新鲜

心无旁骛,沉醉其间

为了利益最大化,学会俯首帖耳

有人侵入你的领地,要明示

闲来常打盹,起前伸懒腰

天天嬉闹玩耍,欢快奔跑

要吸引眼球,任人抚摸

动口不动手,能叫就不咬

煦日暖暖草上躺,四肢好舒展

烈日炎炎多喝水,大树底下好乘凉

开心跳跳,转圈跑跑,全身摇摇

不管苛责有多多

不自责,不噘嘴

回眸一笑泯恩仇

尽享远足的简单快乐

爱吃，爱喝

却适可而止

忠心耿耿

却只做自己

若是想要的深埋地下

只管刨，直到刨到

若是有人哪天不顺心

别说话

静静地依偎

用鼻子轻轻地碰碰他

If a Dog Were Your Teacher

If a dog were your teacher
These are some of the lessons you might learn
When loved ones come home, always run to greet them
Never pass up the opportunity to go for a joy ride
Allow the experience of fresh air and the wind in your face
To be pure ecstasy
When it's in your best interest practice obedience
Let others know when they've invaded your territory
Take naps and stretch before rising
Run romp and play daily
Thrive on attention and let people touch you
Avoid biting, when a simple growl will do
On warm days stop to lie on your back on the grass
On hot days drink lots of water and lay under a shady tree
When you're happy dance around and wag your entire body
No matter how often you're scolded
Don't buy into the guilt thing and pout
Run right back and make friends

Delight in the simple joy of a long walk

Eat with gusto and enthusiasm

Stop when you have had enough

Be loyal

Never pretend to be something you're not

If what you want lies buried

Dig until you find it

When someone is having a bad day

Be silent

Sit close by

And nuzzle them gently

接触的人越多，发现自己越喜欢狗

乔治·格拉汉姆

一个人在世上最好的朋友会与他反目为仇。他悉心养育的儿女会不孝顺。那些和我们最亲近的人，那些我们以幸福和美名相托的人会背信弃义。一个人纵有千金，终能散尽，也许就在他最需要的时候，飞得无影无踪。

一个人会因为一念之差，一时糊涂而名誉扫地。那些当我们功成名就时向我们卑躬屈膝的人，也许是第一个在失败的乌云压顶时对我们落井下石的人。

在这个自私的世界里，人所能拥有的最无私的朋友就是狗，狗对人永远不离不弃，永远不会忘恩负义，永远不会背信弃义。无论富贵还是贫穷，无论是健康还是患病，狗永远与主人形影不离。为了能与主人形影不离，他情愿睡在冰冷的地上，任凭寒风刺骨，雪霜扑面。

即便主人的手里没有狗粮，他也情愿去亲吻。他情愿舔吻艰难世事给主人带来的伤痛。他守护着乞丐主人安眠，如同守护王子。当主人众叛亲离的时候，他不离不弃。当财富不翼而飞，当名誉扫地，他对主人的爱却如日行天际，亘古不变。如果在命运驱使下，主人被世人抛弃，众叛亲离，无家可归，忠诚的狗但求能陪伴主人左右，守卫主人的平安，与主人的敌人搏斗。

当最后的时刻来临，死神拥抱着主人，主人的躯体掩埋在冰冷的地下，虽然所有的朋友都已各奔东西，而在主人的坟墓旁，你会发现看见那条高尚的狗，头伏在两爪之间，眼神悲伤，双眼却警觉地虎视眈眈，继续守卫，忠心耿耿，至死忠心。

A Tribute to the Dog

By George Graham

The best friend a man has in the world may turn against him and become his enemy. His son or daughter that he has reared with loving care may prove ungrateful. Those who are nearest and dearest to us, those whom we trust with our happiness and our good name, may become traitors to their faith. The money that a man has he may lose. It flies away from him, perhaps when he needs it most.

A man's reputation may be sacrificed in a moment of ill-considered action. The people who are prone to fall on their knees to do us honor when success is with us may be the first to throw the stone of malice when failure settles its cloud upon our heads.

The one absolutely unselfish friend that man can have in this selfish world, the one that never deserts him, the one that never proves ungrateful or treacherous, is his dog. A man's dog stands by him in prosperity and in poverty, in health and in sickness. He'll sleep on the cold ground, where the wintry winds blow and the snow drives fiercely, if only he may be near his master's side.

He will kiss the hand that has no food to offer; he will lick the wounds and sores that come from encounter with the roughness of the world. He guards the sleep of his pauper master as if he were a prince. When all other friends desert, he remains. When riches take wings and reputation falls to pieces, he is as constant in his love as the sun in its journeys through the heavens. If fortune drives the master forth, an outcast in the world, friendless and homeless, the faithful dog asks no higher privilege than that of accompanying him, to guard him against danger, to fight against his enemies.

And when the last scene of all comes, and death takes the master in its embrace, and his body is laid away in the cold ground, no matter if all other friends pursue their way, there by the grave will the noble dog be found, his head between his paws, his eyes sad but open in alert watchfulness, faithful and true even in death.

令人难以置信的真实

无论你是否准备好了，总有一天生命会走向尽头。那里不会再有日出，不会再有白昼，不会再有小时或分钟。

你所收集的所有东西，不管是你珍惜的还是遗忘的，终将全部易手他人。

你的怨恨、愤慨、挫折和妒忌也终将不复存在。

同样，你的希望、抱负、计划以及行动日程表也终将全部失效。

当初看得比较重的成败得失也终会消逝无痕。

有人说：人这辈子，一共会死三次。

第一次是当你的心脏停止跳动，那时从生物的角度来看，你死了。

第二次是在为你举行的葬礼上，你的友人纷纷前来吊唁，那时你在社会上的身份死了。

不管是你得到的或是你欠别人的，你的财产、名誉和权势也都会变得无足轻重。

重要的不是你认识多少人，而是在你离开后，有多少人会长时间地感到怅然若失。

第三次是在世界上最后一个记得你的人死了以后，那时你才是真的死了，因为从此以后，再也没有人知道你了。

重要的是别人会记你多长时间，谁记着你，为什么记着你。

因此，趁你还活着，去感受你生命中的方方面面吧：熟悉的陌生、深刻的肤浅、合理的怪异，而其中最重要的是——令人难以置信的真实。你要睁大双眼，屏息静听，尤其要心动不已才对。

The Unbelievably Truth

Ready or not, some day it will all come to an end. There will be no more sunrises, no days, no hours or minutes.

All the things you collected, whether treasured or forgotten, will pass to someone else.

Your grudges, resentments, frustrations, and jealousies will finally disappear.

So, too, your hopes, ambitions, plans, and to-do lists will all expire.

The wins and losses that once seemed so important will fade away.

Someone said during the lifetime of people, a person will die three times in total.

The first time is that when your heart stops beating. Then from the biological perspective, you die.

The second time is that when your friends come to your funeral to hold a memorial ceremony for you, your status in society would deceases at that time.

Your wealth, fame and temporal power will shrivel to

irrelevance. It will not matter what you owned or what you were owed.

What will matter is not how many people you knew, but how many will feel a lasting loss when you're gone.

The third time is that when the last person who remembers you in the world is dead, and then you are really dead for nobody knows you afterwards.

What will matter is how long you will be remembered, by whom and for what.

So when you are still a live, to find in your life the perspectives that are strangely familiar, significantly shallow, reasonably weird, and most importantly, unbelievably true. Keep your eyes wide open, ears sharp and above all the heart beating.

人一辈子能活几次

有一件事是真的：你终有一死。

但有一件事却是假的：人一辈子只能活一次。

一个人成为某一领域的专家，需要 7 年的时间。

那么，倘若你能活到 88 岁的话，在 11 岁之后，你将会有 11 次机会成为伟大的专家。

这就是你的生命历程。

大多数人不愿意就此了断一生。

有些人畏惧死亡。

还有些人认为自己已经是活死人了。

但是，其实，你一生可以活许多次呢。

你可以用一次生命用来写诗。

你还可以用一次生命，来制造点儿什么。

你还可以用一次生命，去寻找事实真相。

事实上，人这一辈子，可以集诗人、发明家、科学家、音乐家、厨师、CEO 于一身，活上一次又一次。

你的生命只有一次，但只要选择得当，一次也就够了。

How Many Lives Do You Have

Here is something true: one day you will be dead.

Here is something false: you only live once.

It takes 7 years to master something.

If you live to be 88, after age 11, you have 11 opportunities to be great at something.

These are your lifetimes.

Most people never let themselves die.

Some are afraid of death.

Some think they are already ghosts.

But you have many lives.

Spend one life writing poems.

Spend another building things.

Spend a life looking for facts.

In fact, one can be a poet, inventor, scientist, musician, cook, CEO all in one during one's lifetime.

You only live once, but if you do it right, once is enough.

我不再想要我的静静

丹尼尔·卡塞米

我的儿子们出生以前,我收到最多的建议是享受现有的寂静时光。等小婴儿一出生,我就永远也不会再找到这样的时光了。与我所听到的许多其他建议不一样的是,这话不幸言中了。

我的大儿子是一个安静的宝宝,他几乎不怎么哭,只是需要我和我丈夫轮流抱着。而我的小儿子出生以后,需要什么的时候却会昭告天下,搞得人人皆知。他从早哭到晚,我很快就晨昏颠倒起来,到了头昏脑涨的地步,有时会出现幻听,从睡梦中醒来,以为他在哭。我机械地做这做那。我对朋友们说如果有人抽我的血,会发现血被咖啡神秘地取代了,他们会哈哈大笑。

最糟糕的是他的哭声会招来他哥哥的哭声。这让我抓狂,我会要我丈夫来帮我,我只有扯开嗓门,才能盖过孩子们的哭声,才能让丈夫听见。左邻右舍没有以为我们天天在吵架,我都很惊讶。

就在我觉得自己再也招架不了的时候,我的两个儿子和丈夫都因为感冒倒下了,他们吃了带催眠成分的药睡着了。我把小儿子放在小床上,慢慢地退出了房间。我终于有了该有的独处时间。我洗了一个热水澡,放松下来。自从小儿子出生以后,我还没有洗过热水澡。半小时以后，我起来走进起居室，读一本这几月来一直想读的书。可是，虽然大家都睡了，我却莫名其妙地无法聚精会神地读书。

我把书放在长沙发上，向我小儿子的小床走去。他在熟睡，嘴微微地张着。我微笑着走出了他的房间，希望不要吵醒他，就回去继续读我的书。书上的字都没有意义，我太分心了，根本读不下去。我飞快地把剩下的几页翻了翻，就合上了。我环顾整个房间，发现地上散落的玩具，水槽里的碗没洗，衣服还没放进洗衣机。我要做的事太多了。只是感觉似乎不对劲儿，出了什么问题。

我打开电视，也许有点儿动静会让我回到正轨。我发现电视节目都很烦人，我不想看。我把电视关掉，继续坐在长沙发上思考。有什么不对头。接着我恍然大悟：家里没动静，没了哭声，没了笑声，没了大呼小叫的声音，只有寂静。

我挨个儿房间去看这些病人。他们都在熟睡。我低头偷偷地看我熟睡的小儿子。接着，我做了一件我也知道不该做的事——我捅了他一下，没有使劲儿捅——只想捅醒他。他稍微动了一下，就又恢复了睡眠状态。我用一根手指滑过他柔嫩的脸蛋儿，想把他弄醒。这次他的反应跟上次一样。我又捅了捅他，捅了四五次，他才真的动弹起来，睁开了双眼，接着，我听到了这个世界上最美妙的声音——他的哭声。

"乖，乖。好啦。妈妈在这儿。"我边把他抱起来边对他说。他立刻止住了哭声又沉沉睡去。这次我把他抱到起居室，坐在他对面，虽然我几乎听不到他的呼吸声，但这个动静对我来说已是足够。

我怀孕的时候，人们说，这样的独处时间以后不会再有了，此言不虚，可是，他们没有认识到的是，我再也不想要这样的独处时间了。

The New Silence

By Danielle Kazemi

Before my sons were born, the most common piece of advice I received was to enjoy the quiet time I had. Once the baby was born, I was never going to get that time again. Unlike many of the other things that I was told, these words were right.

My first son was the quiet baby. He rarely cried, but that may have been from being constantly held by either me or my husband. When my second son was born, though, he was proud to declare to the entire world when he was in need of something. From morning until night, which was quickly becoming a blur to me, he would cry. It got to the point where I could no longer hear myself think, and sometimes I would wake from sleep believing that I was hearing him cry. I was running on automatic. My friends would laugh when I told them that if someone drew my blood, they would find it mysteriously replaced by coffee.

The worst part was that when he would cry, it would make his elder brother cry, too. This would make me fuss with my husband to help me, but I had to raise my voice to an almost shouting level for him to be able to hear me over the crying. I am surprised the neighbors did not think we were fighting with each other every day.

  Just when I thought I couldn't handle any more, my sons and my husband came down with a cold, which caused them to take some medicine that put them to sleep. I placed the baby down in his crib and slowly backed out of the room. Finally, I had the alone time I deserved. I drew myself a warm bath, which I had not had since he was born, and relaxed. After thirty minutes, I got up and went into the living room to read the book I had wanted to read for the past few months. But even though no one else was awake, I wasn't able to concentrate on my book for some reason.

  I placed the book down on the couch and walked over to my baby's crib. He was sleeping with his mouth slightly open. I smiled and walked out of the room, hoping not to wake him, and returned to my book. The words were not making sense to me. I was too distracted to read. I flipped through a few of the remaining pages and closed the book. I looked around the room. There were toys on the ground, plates in the sink, and clothes to be put into the washing-machine. There were plenty of things I could do. It just didn't seem right. There was something wrong.

  I turned on the television. Maybe some noise would help me

to get back on track. I found the television show to be annoying. I didn't want to watch it. I turned it off and continued to sit on the couch and think. Something was out of place. Then it hit me. There was no noise in my house.There was no crying, laughing or yelling at each other. There was just silence.

I went to every room and checked on the patients. They were all asleep. I peered down at my younger son asleep in his crib. Then I did the one thing I knew I should not do—I poked him. Not a hard poke—just enough to wake him up. He stirred for a moment before returning to his slumber state. I ran my finger along his soft cheek, trying to nudge him awake. The same response. So I poked him again. It wasn't until the fourth or fifth poke the started to really move around and open his eyes. Then I heard the most wonderful sound in the world—his cry.

"There, there. It's okay. Mommy's here." I told him as I picked him up. He immediately stopped crying and returned to sleep. This time, I walked with him back into the living room and sat with him against me. Even though I could barely hear it, his breathing was enough noise for me.

People were right when they said that the time I had alone when I was pregnant was never going to happen again. But what they didn't realize is that I wouldn't want it any other way.

山顶小屋

安德鲁·莱特和他的太太要找一个房子,于是去见一个房产经纪人。

"我要到这个城市工作了,"安德鲁对那个房产经纪人说道,"所以我想买个房子。"

"我能帮到你,"房产经纪人答道。"你能出多少钱?"

"不能超过 10000 美元。"安德鲁说道。

"这个城里的房子大部分售价都会高于 10000 美元。"房产经纪人解释道。

"一定要这样才行,"安德鲁的太太解释说。"我们只有两个人,不需要太大的房子。"

房产经纪人看了看他的登记册,"标价 10000 美元的房子我这里只有一个,"他说道。"山顶小屋。"

"房子有什么问题吗?"安德鲁问道。

"那倒没有,"房产经纪人说道。"这是一幢非常好的小屋。"他又看了看他的登记簿。"你们要是喜欢的话,价格可以给你们让到 9000 美元。"

"我不认为你能把这幢房子卖掉。"安德鲁笑着说道。"房子有什么问题?"

"相信我，"房产经纪人说道，"这房子一点儿问题都没有。这是一幢非常好的房子，房前还有大片的鲜花。我不明白我怎么就卖不出去。房子距离城市10公里，不过，如果你们有车的话……"

"哦，我们有车，"珍妮·莱特连忙说，"10公里也不远。再说我也喜欢乡村。"她转向安德鲁，说道，"我们去看看吧。"

"好吧，"安德鲁说道。"看看我们又不会损失什么！"

房产经纪人给了他们几把钥匙。"你们可以自己去吧，是不是？"他说道。"我不能离开办公室。"

他给珍妮和安德鲁讲了讲怎么找到这幢房子，珍妮和安德鲁很快就驱车出了城。他们很快就找到了这幢山顶小屋，山顶小屋果然坐落在山顶。

"哦，我喜欢这幢房子，"他们下车的时候，珍妮感叹道。"看门边的花丛多美呀。"

"我不能理解，"安德鲁说，"为什么就没人住在这里呢？这是一幢非常好的房子，离市区也不远，房子一定有问题。"

他们走到大门前，用钥匙开了门。他们走进房子，房子里非常整洁漂亮。

"哦，安德鲁，"珍妮说道，"我想要的房子就是这样的。对于我们来说正合适。我要上去看看那些卧室。"

她开始往上走。接着，她停下了脚步。"你听到有个声音吗？"她问安德鲁。

安德鲁哈哈大笑。"我想是一只鸟吧。"

"啊，对，"珍妮说道，"那些卧室的窗户也许开了，鸟儿就飞进来了。"她又开始往上走。

"早上好。"

珍妮和安德鲁迅速转过身来，只见一个老头站在大门口。

"你们喜欢这幢房子吗？"他问他们俩。"你们准备买下来吗？"

"我们在考虑买下来。"安德鲁答道。

"很好，"老头说道。"我一周到这里做一次清洁。"

"房产经纪人给的我们钥匙，"珍妮说道，"我正打算去看看那些卧室。"

"啊，好的。"老头说道。"那些卧室。是的。呃，告诉我，你们住在城里吗？"

"哦，不住城里，"珍妮答道。"我们初来乍到。"

"我在城里找到了一份新工作，"安德鲁告诉老头。"所以我们来找一个房子住。"

"啊，是的，"老头说道。"呃，关于这个房子，房产经纪人跟你们说了什么？他告诉过你们这里出过什么事儿吗？"

"没有啊。"安德鲁答道，"他没说。他告诉我们他以前没能把这个房子卖掉，就这些。咦，有什么问题吗？"

"哦，是的，"老头答道。"这房子有问题，这个小屋有问题。不，不。人们不喜欢住在这里，仅此而已。"

"可是为什么呀？"珍妮追问道。

"因为那个姑娘，"老头说道。"一个男人在这里，在一间卧室里，杀死了他的太太。他们都很年轻，像你们一样。"

"哦，不！"珍妮喊道。

"他杀了她，然后把她埋在地下，埋在花丛中，"老头说道。"情况就是这样，可是，警察到现在还没找到她的尸体。"他哈哈大笑，不怀好意的大笑。"可是，她的尸体还在那里。哦，对，她的尸体还在某个地方。人们说她有时候会回来。她走进那间卧室，站在那张床的床边，那张床在……"

"哦,不!"珍妮喊道。"请你不要再说啦。"

"不,这个故事不好听,是吧?"他又哈哈大笑起来。"你们要是把这幢房子买下来的话,我可以帮你们干花园里的活儿。我还可能找到埋在地里的那个姑娘呢。你们永远都无法预料将来会发生什么,是吧?"说完,他转身出了门。

珍妮和安德鲁面面相觑,安德鲁说道,"我不相信这个故事。我们接着去看那些卧室好啦。"

"不,"珍妮说道。"不要看了,安德鲁,不要看了。我也不确定那个故事是真是假,可是我不能住在这里。那个姑娘,她……"

"可是我们花9000美元再也买不到第二套这样的房子啊。"安德鲁劝她。

"对不起,安德鲁,可是我不能住在这里,我会不断地想起……"她用双手捂住了脸。"带我离开这里,安德鲁,求求你。"

她一溜烟儿地从房子里跑了出去,钻进了他们的汽车。安德鲁在后面跟着她。"那我们对房产经纪人怎么解释呢?"他问她。

"哦,对他说这里离城里太远就是了。"她答道。

他们的汽车驶离以后,那个老头再次走进那幢房子。他用钥匙开了门,走了进去。他上楼,走进一间卧室。卧室的地板上有一些旧衣服,还有用旧衣服铺的像床似的东西。一张小小的桌子上有吃的。一个非常苍老的女人坐在桌前。

"他们差点儿上来。"她说道。

"是的,我知道,"老头说。"我差点儿迟到。可是我给他们讲了那个故事,那个女人相信了我。"他哈哈大笑。"女人总是轻信。他们不会再回来了。"

"那就好,"老太太说道。"我们可以再在这里待一两个月了。"

"岂止是一两个月!"老头纠正她。"是一两年好不好!"

The House on the Hill

Andrew Wright and his wife were looking for a house. They went for a house agent.

"I'm coming to work in this town," Andrew told the agent, "and I want buy a house."

"I can help you," the agent said. "How much can you pay?"

"No more than $10,000." Andrew said.

"Most houses in the town are more than $10,000." the agent said.

"There must be something," Andrew's wife said. "We don't want a large house. There are only two of us."

The agent looked in his book. "I've got only one house for $10,000," he said. "Hill House."

"Is there anything the matter with it?" Andrew asked.

"No," the agent said. "It's a very good little house." He looked in his book again. "If you like it, you can have it for $9,000."

"I don't think you can sell it," Andrew said with a

laugh. "What's the matter with it?"

"Believe me," the agent said, "there's nothing the matter with it. It's a very good house and it has lots of flowers in front. I don't know why I can't sell it. It's ten kilometers from the town, but if you have a car..."

"Oh, we've got a car," Jane Wright said, "and ten kilometers isn't far. And I like the country." She turned to Andrew. "Let's go and look at it." she said.

"All right," Andrew said. "What can we lose?"

The house agent gave them some keys. "You can go to the house alone, can't you?" he said. "I must stay in my office."

He told Jane and Andrew how to find the house, and they were soon driving out of the town. They quickly found the Hill House, which stood on the top of a hill.

"Oh, I love this house," Jane said, as they got out of the car. "And look at all the flowers round the door."

"I don't understand this," Andrew said. "Why isn't someone living here? It's a very good house and it's not far from the town. There must be something the matter with it."

They walked to the front door and opened it with the key. They went inside the house. It was very clean and pretty inside.

"Oh, Andrew," Jane said, "this is what I want. It's just right for us. I'm going up to look at the bedrooms."

She began to go up. Then she stopped. "Did you hear a

noise?" she asked Andrew.

Andrew laughed. "I think it was a bird somewhere."

"Ah, yes," Jane said. "A window may be open in one of the bedrooms, and the birds can get in." She began to go up again.

"Good morning."

Jane and Andrew turned quickly. An old man was standing at the front door.

"Do you like this house?" he asked them. "Are you going to buy it?"

"We are thinking about it." Andre said.

"Good," the old man said. "I come here once a week and clean it."

"The agent gave the key," Jane said, "I'm going to look at the bedrooms."

"Ah, yes." the old man said. "The bedrooms. yes. Er, tell me. Do you live in the town?"

"Oh no," Jane said. "We're new here."

"I've got a new job in the town," Andrew told him. "So we're looking for a house."

"Ah yes," the old man said. "Er, what did the agent tell you about the house? Did he tell you what happened here?"

"No." Andrew said, "he didn't. He told us he couldn't sell the house, that's all. Why? Is there something the matter with it?"

"Oh no," the old man said. "There's something matter with the house, with the building. No, no. People don't like to live here. that's all."

"But why not?" Jane asked.

"Because of the girl," the old man said. "A man killed his wife here. In one of the bedrooms. They were both young. Like you."

"Oh no!" Jane cried.

"He killed her and put her under the ground, among the flowers," the old man said. "That's the story, but the police never found her." He laughed. It was not a nice laugh. "But she's there. Oh, yes, she's there somewhere. People say she comes back to the house sometimes. She goes to the bedroom and stands near the bed—the bed where—"

"Oh no!" Jane cried. "Please don't say any more."

"No, it's not a nice story, is it?" He laughed again. "If you buy the house I can work for you in the garden. I may even find the girl in the ground. You never know, do you?" He turned and walked out of the door.

Jane and Andrew looked at each other, and then Andrew said, "I don't believe that story. Let's go and look at the bedrooms."

"No," Jane said. "No, Andrew, no. I don't know if the

story is true or not, but I can't live here. That girl, she—"

"But we can't find another house for only $9,000." Andrew said.

"I'm sorry, Andrew, but I can't live here. I shall always think about..." She put her face in her hands. "Take me away from here, Andrew. Please."

She ran out of the house and got into the car. Andrew walked after her. "What shall we tell the agent?" he asked her.

"Oh, tell him it's too far from the town." she said.

As the car moved away, the old man walked back into the house. He opened the door with a key and went inside. He went up into one of the bedrooms. There were some old clothes on the floor. There was a kind of bed made from old clothes. There was food on a small table. A very old woman was sitting at the table.

"They nearly came up," she said.

"Yes, I know," the old man said. "I was nearly late. But I told them the story. The woman believed me." He laughed. "The women always do. They won't be back."

"Good," the old woman said. "We can stay here for another month or two."

"Month or two!" the old man said, "Another year or two!"

图书在版编目（CIP）数据

所有的路　最终都是回家的路：英汉对照/（美）约瑟夫·伍德·克鲁奇等著；张白桦译.—北京：中国国际广播出版社，2018.4（2019.1重印）
（译趣坊.世界微型小说精选）
ISBN 978-7-5078-4275-3

Ⅰ.①所… Ⅱ.①约…②张… Ⅲ.①小小说－小说集－美国－现代－英、汉 Ⅳ.①I712.45

中国版本图书馆CIP数据核字（2018）第065151号

所有的路　最终都是回家的路（中英双语）

著　　者	[美]约瑟夫·伍德·克鲁奇 等
译　　者	张白桦
策　　划	张娟平
责任编辑	笑学婧
版式设计	国广设计室
责任校对	徐秀英

出版发行	中国国际广播出版社 [010-83139469 010-83139489（传真）]
社　　址	北京市西城区天宁寺前街2号北院A座一层
	邮编：100055
网　　址	www.chirp.com.cn
经　　销	新华书店
印　　刷	环球东方（北京）印务有限公司

开　　本	880×1230　1/32
字　　数	200千字
印　　张	6.75
版　　次	2018年5月　北京第一版
印　　次	2019年1月　第二次印刷
定　　价	26.00元

欢迎关注本社新浪官方微博
官方网站 www.chirp.cn

版权所有
盗版必究